Fervent Faith

Discover how a fervent spirit
is a defense against the devil.

Jennifer LeClaire
Author of *Faith Magnified and Breakthrough!*

Fervent Faith: Discover How a Fervent Spirit is a Defense Against the Devil

ISBN: 978-0-9819795-2-6

Published by Jennifer LeClaire Ministries

P.O. Box 3953

Hallandale Beach, Fla. 33008

305-467-4284

www.jenniferleclaire.org

DEDICATION

I dedicate this book to the saints of days gone by; those men and women of God who left us an living example of what it truly means to be on fire for God.

TABLE OF CONTENTS

PREFACE

Remember the last time you needed a breakthrough? You were desperate. You pastor couldn't help you. Your best friend couldn't help you. Not even your momma could help you. The only possible way to get a breakthrough was for God to do the impossible.

But you had faith. You knew that with God all things are possible to him that believes. You knew that what's impossible for man is possible with God. You knew that God was still on the throne and hears and answers prayers.

So what did you do? You confessed the Word. You rejoiced in the trial. You called those things that be not as though they were and you thanked Him. You meditated on the Word day and night waiting for the good success. You prayed and prayed – and then you prayed some more with all the fervency you could muster. You sought God with everything in you, trusting Him to heal your body, deliver you from trouble, meet your need, mend your relationship, save your child...

Then you got the breakthrough. You rejoiced in the Lord for day or two or three. And before you even realized it, somewhere on your mountaintop, your fire started to wane. And before too long, the devil was attacking you in that same place. Your symptoms started coming back, trouble visited again, you were faced with a dire need, your relationships were in a mess, your child was backsliding…And you were desperate for another breakthrough. You went from a spiritual high to an emotional low faster than a rollercoaster races down the rails that carry it.

But it didn't have to be that way. If we maintained the fervency we displayed when we were seeking the God of the breakthrough, we could have continued to walk in the victory that belongs to us instead of walking in emotional defeat. Don't beat yourself up. Even Elijah the miracle-working prophet, once fell into spiritual slump. Of course, he got back up again – and so must we.

I wrote this book because too many of us get desperate when we need a breakthrough, then lose our glow when the miracle manifests. Instead of letting the answers to prayer propel us to new depths in Him, we return to the surface; to life as usual. My brethren, it need not be this way. We can maintain spiritual fervency at all times – and that fervency will carry us through the hills and valleys without the spiritual highs and the emotional lows.

My prayer is that this book will ignite something in you – a stronger zeal for Christ – that you can then spread to others. Like a wildfire in the spirit, may this book be the catalyst for stirring your faith, your passion, your fervency to new heights in Him. Amen.

CHAPTER 1
Fervent in Spirit

*Be kindly affectioned one to another with brotherly love; in
honour preferring one another; Not slothful in business; fervent
in spirit; serving the Lord; Rejoicing in hope; patient in
tribulation; continuing instant in prayer...*

Romans 12:10-12

Everybody is standing to their feet. Some are praying.
Others are clapping. Still others are euphoric. The
atmosphere is energized. The crowd is unified. You
can feel the expectation in the air...It's as if at any
moment there could be an explosive celebration.

Unfortunately, the scene I just described isn't your
typical American church service – it's your typical
American sporting event.

I'll never forget the time I was watching the Boston Celtics play in an NBA playoff game. The scene was intense. It was game seven. Win or go home. Everything depended on what would happen in the next couple of minutes. When the camera swept the crowd, I say people praying, clapping, cheering – and praying some more. In other words, I saw fervency.

Nobody was worried about the turkey in the oven back home. Nobody was thinking about the list of errands they had to run after the game. Nobody was thinking about the pain in their body. Everybody's attention was on the basketball court, almost as if their life depended on the outcome of the next 2:48. The crowd wouldn't let anything distract them from seeing the victory for which they were hoping and believing.

You've heard the analogy before. People stand up and shout for their favorite sports team but they don't always stand up and shout for their God. They'll passionately defend their child's right to a "B" instead of a "C" to a fair-minded schoolteacher who probably should have given the kid a "D." But they aren't as passionate about defending their Father's Word in the marketplace when a foul-mouthed co-worker speaks against Jesus.

Now don't get me wrong. I'm not against a good game. I enjoy watching passionate people perform at high levels. I would just like to see more Christians display the same zeal about their Savior as they do about their Sports. After all, the Bible doesn't say to be fervent in sports, serving the world. It says to be fervent in spirit, serving the Lord. And it's not just sports. We can just as easily misplace our fervency with any dumb idol. We should enjoy our hobbies, but not more than we enjoy our God.

GOD'S FERVENT EXPECTATION

A fervent spirit is visible, and you can't fake it 'till you make it in the Kingdom of God. God knows our hearts, and He expects them to be on fire for Him. So, ask yourself this question: Am I fervent in spirit?

If you had to stop and think about it for too long, then the answer is probably no. If you answered too quickly without thinking about it at all, then take some time to examine yourself before you offer your final answer.

Here's why: You may think you are fervent in spirit, but when you look at the fruit of your life you may decide you need to separate the wheat from the chaff. You may need the fire of God to burn away some impurities and reset you on the path of passion.

It can happen to any of us if we're not careful. I can remember times when I got so caught up in the work of the ministry that I approached burn out rather than approaching God with a burning heart. I can also remember times when I was overwhelmed by my circumstances instead of being overwhelmed by His goodness. This grieves the Spirit of God – and it demonstrates wrong priorities. We have to seek first the Kingdom of God and His righteousness – and we need to do it with hearts ablaze.

Don't get mad at me. I'm not the one with the expectation – God is. God expects us to be fervent. It's a command. It's a theme that runs through the Bible and is especially manifest in the Book of Acts. Where you see fervency, you see salvations. Where you see fervency, you see miracles. Where you see fervency, you see deliverance. Where you see fervency, you see the spirit of Christ showing up on the scene to work with those who believe.

So, I ask you again? Are you truly fervent in spirit? Are you on fire for God? Do you love Him with all your heart and with all your soul and with all your mind and with all your strength? (Matthew 12:30). When one of the scribes asked Jesus which is the most important commandment, that was His answer. The most important commandment is to love God with everything in you. When you do, it will manifest in the form of a fervent faith that everyone can see.

STOKING THE FIRE

Maybe you aren't as fervent as you thought you were. Maybe you can agree that God expects us to be fervent, but you don't know how to stoke your fire. Maybe you halfway gave up a long time ago. Maybe your once-roaring fire is merely smoldering in the wake of one trial after another. Maybe you get a glimmer of hope thinking about what your life could be like if you were on fire for God, but you just can't seem to crossover from on-again-off-again seeking to full-force, nothing's-gonna-stop-you pursuit of God Almighty in all His glory.

Listen, it's OK. I know how you feel. If you are reading this book, then I have good news for you: The Holy Spirit is going to help you fan the flames of your first love. He's going to help you rekindle your fire. If your heart's desire is to be fervent in spirit, serving the Lord, He's going to give you the desires of your heart.

If you are already on fire for God, keep reading. God's going to help you maintain the glow and use you as a vessel to spread that fire to those in need of a salvation and a fresh anointing from the Holy Ghost. He's going to use you as an example to others of what true zeal for the Lord looks like in action. If your heart's desire is to burn and shine, He's going to give you the desires of your heart.

If you want to keep your deliverance, if you want to keep your healing, if you want to keep your breakthrough, if you want to live in victory, if you want to reach your destiny, if you want to help somebody – you need to maintain a fervent spirit. A fervent spirit is your defense against the devil. It's your guard against apathy. It's your protection against lukewarmness.

FERVENCY, PASSION, ZEAL – AND YOU

Before we take one step further, we need to take a moment to examine what fervency is and what God has to say about it.

Merriam-Webster defines the word "fervent" as very hot or glowing. When something is fervent, it is "exhibiting or marked by a great intensity or feeling." Let's drill down a little deeper to the roots of the word. The English word "fervency" comes from the Greek word "zeo." It literally means "to boil."

Can you imagine? Have you ever watched water boil? It bubbles up with utter intensity – and sometimes it even escapes the confines of the pot. Boiling water can't hide its expression. In fact, if you come too close to a pot of boiling water, the steam alone will get your attention.

Noteworthy is the fact that boiling is a way to purify water. As we are boiling over for God, I believe our souls are being purified. Think about it for a minute. We won't be consumed with demonic imaginations when we are consumed with a godly focus. There is no devilish playground in the fervent spirit.

A fervent spirit is on fire for God. A fervent spirit is a passionate spirit. A fervent spirit is a zealous spirit. God likes fervency. Again, He expects us to be fervent in spirit. The Bible has plenty to say about fervency. The Holy Spirit started to use the word "fervency" in the Book of Acts.

A FRESH ANOINTING

We can't be fervent without the Holy Ghost. That's why the Apostle Paul admonishes us to "be not drunk with wine, wherein is excess; but be filled with the Spirit" (Ephesians 5:18). In the Greek, the phrase "be filled" literally means to "be being filled" with the Spirit, signaling the need to be continually filled with the Holy Ghost.

Maybe you need a fresh anointing right now. Jesus, the one who baptizes us in the Holy Ghost, promised that if you hunger and thirst after righteousness, you shall be filled (Matthew 5:6). There was no expiration date on that promise.

If you need a fresh touch of His anointing, you don't have to tarry. Just ask and receive that your joy may be full – and that you may be full of the Holy Ghost. Be being filled. The Apostle Paul wouldn't have issued this mandate to the church at Ephesus if it wasn't vital to Christian living.

I don't see how one can maintain a fervent spirit – a spirit that is on fire for God with an all-consuming passion that drives every move – without being filled with the Spirit. The Bible clearly states that apart from Him we can do nothing (John 15:5).

Jesus sent the Holy Spirit to be our Helper. He'll help you stay fervent in spirit if you let Him. By contrast, when you quench His spirit, I believe you also quench your own spirit, for He is the one who stirs within you a passion for the Christ and for the Father.

FERVENT FAITH

What does the Bible say about fervency? Plenty. We see fervency in action in the Book of Acts time and time again. In the early Church, we saw such fervency that people were willing to sacrifice their time, their money and their lives to serve the Lord and advance His Kingdom.

Oh, that we saw this fervent spirit in the Church more often today rather than the apathetic and lukewarm spirit that allows the flesh, the world and the devil to have its way. When the Lord returns, will he find fervent faith in the earth? The Bible specifically talks about fervency in several contexts:

- Being fervent in spirit (Romans 12:11)
- Being fervent in mind (2 Corinthians 7:7)
- Laboring fervently in prayer (Colossians 4:12; James 5:16)
- Loving one another fervently (1 Peter 1:22; 1 Peter 4:8)

Later in the book we're going to take the fervency test. In the meantime, begin to examine your heart. As you see examples of fervency peppered throughout this text, consider whether your life displays these passions. When you consider that fervency is a mandate for the Christian and a defense against the devil, you'll begin to desire to burn and shine for the Lord. And God will give you the desires of your heart as you seek Him.

FERVENT IN DEED

Faith without works is dead (James 2:20). Like Abraham, our faith and our actions must work together. Our faith is made complete by what we do. Fueled by a fervent spirit, fervent faith always demonstrates fervent deeds.

When the Holy Ghost filled the 120 people gathered in the upper room waiting on the promise of the Father, they became so fervent in spirit that people thought they were drunk. Many disciples were so fervent in spirit they sold their possessions and lay the money at the apostles' feet.

Stephen was so fervent in spirit that he confronted the religious rulers of the day and forgave them even as he was being stoned to death. Peter's disciples were so fervent in spirit they prayed without ceasing until an angel delivered him from his cell (Acts 12:5).

Epaphras is a lesser-known example of fervent faith, but a powerful example indeed. Epaphras was an intercessor that understood, even before the Apostle James penned it by the Holy Ghost, that the effective fervent prayer of a righteous man makes tremendous power available (James 5:16). Look what the Apostle Paul wrote about him:

> Epaphras, who is one of you, a servant of Christ, saluteth you, always labouring fervently for you in prayers, that ye may stand perfect and complete in all the will of God. For I bear him record, that he hath a great zeal for you, and them that are in Laodicea, and them in Hierapolis.
>
> Colossians 4:12-14

Of course, you remember Nehemiah's charge to rebuild the wall. As he records the rebuilding process, Nehemiah calls out Baruch in particular. While Jedaiah, Hattush, Shallum, Hanun, Malkijah and many others were mentioned for their work in rebuilding the wall and its gates, Baruch was specifically called out as one who worked zealously (Nehemiah 3:20 NIV). Baruch had a different spirit and it manifested in his work. Incidentally, the name Baruch means "blessed." When we do the work of the Lord, we mustn't merely show up with a good attitude. People should see our fervency in spirit, serving the Lord. They should be blessed by witnessing our fervency.

God Almighty Himself is characterized by zeal. Over and over again in the Old Testament we see references to the zeal of the Lord. The zeal of God sometimes manifests as the fire of God (Isaiah 26:11);

sometimes as affection (Isaiah 63:15). The point is that God is a passionate God. He's passionate about His Word and He's passionate about His people. When we are zealous for God, we will be anxious to defend His Word and His people – and His honor.

ZEAL THAT CONSUMES

Your zealous actions speak louder than your positive confession. We need both, of course. I'm not dunning a positive confession. The point is you can say you are fervent in spirit, but if you don't go to church, if you don't pray, if you don't study your Bible to show yourself approved, if you don't share Christ with others, if you don't let your fire burn and shine among men, then how fervent are you, really?

Zeal is visible. Jehu said, "Come and see my zeal for the Lord" and slew all that remained of the house of Ahab, according to the word of Elijah (2 Kings 10:16). You could see his zeal. The zeal of the Lord's house should consume us (Psalm 69:9). The Apostle Paul said the zeal of the believers in the church at Corinth stirred up others (2 Corinthians 9:2). And Paul told his spiritual son Titus that Jesus gave Himself for us, that He might redeem us all from iniquity, and purify unto Himself a peculiar people, zealous of good works (Titus 2:14). The Lord expects us to have a zealous faith that's visible to the whole world.

Does your fervent life, boldness and ability to rightly divide the Word of Truth convince folks that Jesus was the Lamb of God who came to save the world from an eternal hellfire? If not, it's time to stir up the gift of God within you. God needs you. The world is waiting for you to manifest His glory. God is ready to anoint you and send you into your high calling.

CHAPTER 2
Your Spiritual Defense

*For he put on righteousness as a breastplate, and an helmet of
salvation upon his head; and he put on the garments of
vengeance for clothing, and was clad with zeal as a cloak.*

Isaiah 59:17

A fervent spirit is a defense against the devil. In fact,
zeal is part of our spiritual armor. Remember,
fervency, zeal and passion run together. Where you
find one, you'll find the other. It's impossible to be
fervent without displaying passion. It's impossible to
be zealous without a fervent spirit. It's impossible to
fulfill your destiny without an all-consuming passion
for His will. I believe that's why Jesus said,

"Enter through the narrow gate; for wide
is the gate and spacious and broad is the

way that leads away to destruction, and many are those who are entering through it. But the gate is narrow (contracted by pressure) and the way is straitened and compressed that leads away to life, and few are those who find it."

Matthew 7:13-14

Think about it for a minute. The narrow gate is contracted by pressure. What kind of pressure? The pressure that demands we crucify our flesh with its affections and lusts (Galatians 5:24). The pressure that conforms us into the image of Christ (Romans 8:29). The pressure that changes us into His image from glory to glory, even as by the Spirit of the Lord (2 Corinthians 3:17-18).

There have been times when I could literally feel the pressure of that narrow path crushing the self-life that hindered me. Times when the force of life's circumstances bore down on my soul to the point of what felt like death. And it was death. It was death to self. I've broken bones and birthed babies, and I am convinced the pain that comes with dying to self is the most intense. But it's this pain, this pressure, that brings forth the fruit of spiritual maturity.

A fervent spirit is zealous for the Lord and passionate about His work even during the process of dying to self. In fact, dying to self is so much easier when we have fervent faith, when we can see the end of the process in the midst of it. Then we can truly rejoice in the fiery trial. Then we have an upper hand on the wicked one.

Spiritual zeal is an intense pursuit of the Kingdom of God and His righteousness at all times. It's a mantle that covers us with a bold anointing to confront those things that oppose the Gospel, even when those things are within us. It's a divine passion that burns in your spirit when you are consumed with the fire of the living God.

OUR SPIRITUAL ARMOR

Again, a fervent spirit is a defense against the devil. In fact, zeal is part of our armor. Often times, we rely on the Holy Spirit-inspired words of the Apostle Paul to better understand our the weapons of our warfare, which are not carnal but mighty through God to the pulling down of strongholds (2 Corinthians 10:4). We also draw upon his Holy Ghost wisdom shared in the sixth chapter of the Book of Ephesians. Let's review that now:

> Finally, my brethren, be strong in the Lord, and in the power of his might. Put on the whole armour of God, that ye may be able to stand against the wiles of the devil.
>
> For we wrestle not against flesh and blood, but against principalities, against

powers, against the rulers of the darkness of this world, against spiritual wickedness in high places. Wherefore take unto you the whole armour of God, that ye may be able to withstand in the evil day, and having done all, to stand.

Stand therefore, having your loins girt about with truth, and having on the breastplate of righteousness; And your feet shod with the preparation of the gospel of peace; Above all, taking the shield of faith, wherewith ye shall be able to quench all the fiery darts of the wicked. And take the helmet of salvation, and the sword of the Spirit, which is the word of God:

Praying always with all prayer and supplication in the Spirit, and watching thereunto with all perseverance and supplication for all saints...

Ephesians 6:10-18

I've read my fair share of teachings on Ephesians 6:10-18. Indeed, there is a lot of helpful revelation that men and women of God have drawn from these verses. Recently when I read these verses, though, a few things leaped from the black and white pages and into my fervent spirit.

WHY YOU NEED THE WHOLE ARMOR

First of all, I have good news. You don't need to invest in armor. It doesn't cost you a dime to acquire this heavy duty battle gear. Jesus paid the price for us to have it – but it's up to us to put it on.

If you neglect to put on the whole armor – if you leave the house without your shoes of peace because you were too busy arguing with your wife, husband, sister, brother, child or fill-in-the-blank – then you have left yourself vulnerable to the wicked one. If you disregard any piece of your battle array you are open to attack.

Think of it this way: Each element of your armor works with the others to offer complete protection in the face of spiritual opposition. The very word "armor" suggests an assembly of parts, not a single piece. How can your faith work without the belt of truth? It can't. Your faith is activated by hearing the Word of Truth. How can your faith work without the breastplate of righteousness? It can't. Without a revelation of your righteousness coming from Christ, the devil will successfully drag you into the pit of self-condemnation every time you make the slightest mistake. The Sword of the Spirit, which is the Word of God, won't work for you if you don't wield it in faith.

Consider the seven sons of Sceva. Sceva was a Jew and a chief of the priests. As such, his sons were educated in the Word of God. They took it upon themselves to try to cast out evil spirits, saying, "We adjure you by Jesus whom Paul preacheth" (Acts 19:13). The only problem was, these seven sons of Sceva didn't have faith in the Word of God made flesh. In other words, they didn't have faith in Jesus and had no basis on which to exercise His authority. They didn't have a relationship with Him. They were not born-again. The devils knew they had no authority to use the name. Let's look at the fate of these young men:

> And the evil spirit answered and said, Jesus I know, and Paul I know; but who are ye? And the man in whom the evil spirit was leaped on them, and overcame them, and prevailed against them, so that they fled out of that house naked and wounded.

> Acts 19:15-16

Now let me ask you this. Do you think these seven sons of Sceva were wearing the armor of God? I submit to you that if they had been, the outcome of this spiritual confrontation would have been much different. But these sons of Sceva didn't even have the helmet of salvation, much less the breastplate of righteousness or their feet shod with the Gospel of peace.

When you are fervent in spirit, you will not neglect to spend the time it takes to put on the whole armor of

God each morning. You know you are in a war with unseen spiritual forces – and you are humble enough to know that you can't overcome in your own strength.

If you are a born-again believer, you already have authority. Jesus gave it to you (Luke 10:19-29). Fervent faith in the Lord Jesus Christ, His Word and His name – a fervent spirit – is what gives you the strength to wield the sword. It's the fervency that puts the pep in our step. If your faith isn't extremely and determinedly intense, the devil will use fear to defeat you. Faith and fear are spiritual opponents.

WHEN YOUR SHIELD BEGINS TO SLIP

I've heard people say their arms sometimes grow tired of holding up the shield of faith; that it gets so heavy they are tempted to put it down. I know the feeling. I think we've all been there. That doesn't mean you aren't fervent. It just means you need some back up.

Jesus sent the apostles out two and two. He doesn't expect us to fight every battle alone. The Bible says one can put a thousand to flight but two can put 10,000 to flight when the Lord is on our side (Deuteronomy 32:30) .

Don't let the devil lie to you. Moses had a fervent spirit, didn't he? Yet, he grew weary in battle. So when you feel like giving up, when physical exhaustion creeps in, when you can't see an end in sight, fall back on wisdom: call for help.

> Moses said to Joshua, "Choose men for us and go out, fight against Amalek Tomorrow I will station myself on the top of the hill with the staff of God in my hand." Joshua did as Moses told him, and fought against Amalek; and Moses, Aaron, and Hur went up to the top of the hill.
>
> So it came about when Moses held his hand up, that Israel prevailed, and when he let his hand down, Amalek prevailed.
>
> But Moses' hands were heavy. Then they took a stone and put it under him, and he sat on it; and Aaron and Hur supported his hands, one on one side and one on the other. Thus his hands were steady until the sun set. So Joshua overwhelmed Amalek and his people with the edge of the sword.
>
> Exodus 17:9-13 (NASB)

If you are on the Lord's side, that means we're all in this together. Joshua couldn't have defeated the Amalekites if Moses wasn't dedicated to holding up the staff of God. But Moses couldn't have continued holding up his arms if Aaron and Hur hadn't supported him in the cause. Don't wait until the devil has you in a corner before you call for help.

Remember, you are in a war with unseen spiritual forces – and you need to be humble enough to know that you can't overcome in your own strength. In all instances that means relying on God, but in some cases that also means relying on other fervent spiritual warriors who can join forces with you to bring God's will to pass in your life or in a situation.

24/7/365 FERVENCY

Before we get off the topic of the whole armor of God, I want to point out one more thing. You can't wait until it's time to go to war to stir up your passion. You need to be fervent in spirit 24/7/365. Remember, fervency is a defense against the devil.

I can guarantee you this: The devil is fervent about his ministry and he's managed to impassion thousands of evil spirits – spirits that once enjoyed the very presence of the God who created them – that rejoice when your zeal wanes. These wicked ones are actively working to lead you away from God's plan for your life into the fiery inferno that is hell itself. Consider the Apostle Peter's warning:

> Be well balanced (temperate, sober of mind), be vigilant and cautious at all times; for that enemy of yours, the devil, roams around like a lion roaring in fierce

hunger], seeking someone to seize upon and devour. Withstand him; be firm in faith [against his onset--rooted, established, strong, immovable, and determined]…

1 Peter 5:8-9 (AM)

I like the Amplified translation of these verses because it both demonstrates the intensity of the devil – a lion in fierce hungry to destroy – and the intensity of the believer who withstands him – established, strong, immovable and determined. That, my brothers and sisters, is fervent faith.

While the enemy is hungry for our souls, we should be hungry for God's righteousness. Jesus promised that those who hunger and thirst after righteousness shall be filled (Matthew 5:6). Filled with what? Filled with His righteousness, filled with His spirit, filled with the God kind of faith. When we're fervent, we stay filled and the devil will go hunting for prey somewhere else.

PREPARING FOR BATTLE

Again, you have to prepare for battle. Let's look at Ephesians 6:10-18 through that lens. We're going to read from the New Living Translation because it draws it out in plainer language without losing Paul's original intent:

A final word: Be strong in the Lord and in his mighty power. Put on all of God's armor so that you will be able to stand firm against all strategies of the devil.

For we are not fighting against flesh-and-blood enemies, but against evil rulers and authorities of the unseen world, against mighty powers in this dark world, and against evil spirits in the heavenly places.

Therefore, put on every piece of God's armor so you will be able to resist the enemy in the time of evil. Then after the battle you will still be standing firm. Stand your ground, putting on the belt of truth and the body armor of God's righteousness. For shoes, put on the peace that comes from the Good News so that you will be fully prepared.

In addition to all of these, hold up the shield of faith to stop the fiery arrows of the devil. Put on salvation as your helmet, and take the sword of the Spirit, which is the word of God.

Ephesians 6:10-18 (NLT)

First, Paul says we have to put on all of God's armor so we can stand against the devil. The helmet of salvation alone isn't going to offer victory. In other words, getting saved and waiting to get to heaven isn't the end all. God expects you to be fervent in spirit, serving Him, all the days of your life. There is no retirement in the Kingdom of God, but you don't have to wait until you are 65 to collect your benefits, either (Psalm 103). If you are doing the will of God, that means you are going to get some spiritual opposition from age-old devils who don't want to see you do anything great in the name of the Lord. But this is your destiny in Christ. So you need to get prepared for battle.

Now, consider the words "having" and "taking" in the context of these verses. The Apostle Paul said "having" three pieces of the armor: the belt of truth, the breastplate of righteousness, and the shoes of the preparation of the Gospel of peace. He then talks about "taking" three pieces of the armor: the shield of faith, the helmet of salvation and the sword of the spirit.

There's a shift that takes place between the having and the taking. I believe the "having" is the preparation. The Bible speaks of preparing for war (Joel 3:9). In the Old Testament, they fought literal battles. In the New Testament, we fight spiritual wars. Preparing means meditating on the truth at all times, meditating on our position in Christ as the righteousness of God and seeking His righteousness in our daily lives, and learning how to hold our peace in every situation. This is God's will for us and if we do these things fervently, they serve as a defense against the devil. These are some of the ways we prepare for war. It's been said burglars look for the easy wins, the open doors, the unprepared targets. The same holds true of the devil. Preparing for war, in and of itself, is a devil deterrent.

Listen, you can't wait until the war is raging to get prepared. You need to get and stay prepared at all times because you may not always know when the enemy is going to attack your finances, when he's going to attack your health, when he's going to attack your relationships—when he's going to attack whatever.

If you aren't prepared when the attack comes, the enemy is likely to get in a few blows before you are fully dressed for battle. That's not God's will for you. He already defeated the devil, but we need to enforce that victory in our own lies. If the devil can deceive us, he can gain a foothold in our circumstances.

ENGAGING THE ENEMY

We need to be prepared, but we can't spend our whole lives just getting prepared. Sooner or later, the time comes when we have to engage the enemy in order to enforce God's will in our lives. The time comes when we have to run to the battle line to confront the giant that's hindering God's plan. The time may even come when God calls us into active duty at ground zero to intercede for another who needs back up in the battle.

There are certain pieces of armor that we put on as we prepare for war. And there are other pieces we take with us as we enter the battle. Again, we prepare through study and meditation on God's Word, seeking His face and holding our peace. But we head to the battle line with the helmet of salvation to combat the thoughts that come against our minds. We pick up the shield of faith to block all the circumstantial darts of the enemy. And we speak the Spirit-inspired, Spirit-empowered Word of God out of our mouths to stop the devil dead in his tracks. And we do it all fervently, defending His honor, bringing Him glory, advancing His causes, helping His creation. It's all about Jesus. It's His armor and His battle.

Unlike Saul's armor that was too big for David in the battle against Goliath, God's armor fits us like the proverbial glove. We just have to put it on – and we have to learn how to use it the right way. Just as your natural shoes need to be tied to stay on your feet, your shoes of peace must be worn properly. You can't kick them off when someone ticks you off, nor can you cover them up when you don't want anyone to see you wearing them. In other words, you can't stop sharing the Gospel of peace because you fear the backlash. There is power in the Gospel, and if you deny that power for fear of man, how can your feet be prepared, as the Amplified Bible says, "to face the enemy with the firm-footed stability, the promptness, and the readiness produced by the good news of the Gospel of peace"? (Ephesians 6:15) We need to both learn how to use our armor and refuse to compromise its integrity.

THE ARMOR OF LIGHT

We'll talk more about the whole armor in a minute because there's even more to it than we are typically taught—and it's awesome. But right now I want to make sure we understand another piece of the armor that we don't talk about much. Beyond the armor outlined in Ephesians 6, Paul also mentions the armor of light (Romans 13:12). We could do an entire study on light, but for the purposes of understanding our armor, I want to focus only on the context of this one Scripture and what it practically means for you and me.

What does it mean to put on the armor of light? It's important to understand because I think while we're getting spiritually dressed each morning, lacing our shoes of peace, buckling our belt of truth, fitting our breastplate of righteousness, and straightening our helmet of salvation, I think we sometimes forget to put on the armor of light.

The Bible says God is Light, and in Him is no darkness at all (1 John 1:5). The Bible also says Jesus was the true Light (John 1:8). Some thought John the Baptist was the Light. The Prophet John was not the Light, but he was anointed as a burning and shining light (John 5:35). Like John the Baptist, we are not the Light, but Jesus said we are the light of the world (Matthew 5:14). Jesus was the light of the world when

He walked the earth (John 8:12). We are children of light because we believe in the light (John 12:36). God is the Father of lights (James 1:7).

Just as Jesus gave us His authority to wield in the earth for His glory, He also gave us His life, which is the light of men (John 9:5; John 1:4). So, again, what does it mean to put on the armor of light? I believe it means to put on Jesus Himself, the Light. The Apostle Paul instructed us to put on the Lord Jesus Christ, making no provision for the flesh to fulfill the lusts thereof (Romans 13:13). Christ is our armor of Light. When you are truly wearing your armor of Light, it's blinding to the devil, who prefers to walk in darkness in his hunt for someone to devour. Where there is darkness in us, there is an opening for the devil to operate. The armor of light is a defense against the devil.

Now, just because you are saved doesn't mean you are automatically wearing the armor of Light. You have to make a conscious choice to put on Christ every day, just like you have to make a conscious decision to die to self every day. You have to clothe yourself with Christ every morning, just like you have to clothe yourself with natural clothes every morning. Like Joyce Meyer has said, your clothes aren't going to jump out of your closet and on to your body. You have to make a decision and an effort. Failing to put on Christ is like running around spiritually naked. The devils will point and laugh at the scene, then seize the opportunity to attack.

IMITATING CHRIST'S CHARACTER

Next question: What does it mean to put on Christ? Charles Finney offers light on the topic that we need to recall in today's darkened society. Finney was a 19th Century Presbyterian minister who became a central figure in the second Great Awakening. Some call him "The Father of Modern Revivalism."

As Finney saw it, putting on Christ is to assume His character, and peculiarities, as an actor does on the stage. The commandment, he preached, means to imitate Christ. But it's more than mere imitation in the dramatic sense of the world. Let's listen in on one of his lectures based on Romans 13:13, offered on March 15, 1843:

> It implies the putting away of selfishness. Christ was not selfish. Selfishness is the preference of self-gratification, to the will of God, and the good of the universe, and Christ never did this. The Apostle adds, 'and make no provision for the flesh, to fulfill the lusts thereof.' Here, he contrasts 'putting on Christ,' and 'making provision for the flesh,' which is the same as selfishness. Paul was more philosophical than any of the sacred writers, and employs the language – 'works of the flesh,' 'following after the flesh,' 'carnal mind,' to designate the nature of sin. But the whole Bible

condemns self-seeking as wrong, and inconsistent with the true service of God, or imitation of Christ.

It implies living for the same end for which Christ lived. What was His end? Not the gratification of self, but the well-being of the universe, and whoever puts Him on must adopt the same end. It implies the same singleness of eye. Christ's eye was not double, but exclusively directed to one end, the glory of God. It implies such a sympathy with Him, as to beget an imitation of Him. A profound sympathy is necessary to, and naturally begets imitation.

HOW TO PUT ON CHRIST

Thank God, Finney didn't leave his listeners without a how-to. Today, we have the benefit of His wisdom and study of Scripture to outline for us what he believed were nine essential steps to obeying this command to put on Christ. We can begin here with our own study and practice. Let's take a bunny trail of sorts and review Finney's nine steps here:

1. Study His Character: A deep and intense study of His character, until the great principle of His action is clearly perceived – the real idea of the end for which He lived clearly developed. To represent Christ we must catch His spirit, and make His grand end and aim ours. Then we shall act as He would under like circumstances.

2. Believe the Word: You must fully believe that through grace you can put Him on. While you don't believe you can, of course you cannot. No one can intend to do what he believes he cannot do. It is absurd to suppose the contrary. Unless you believe you can put on Christ, it is utterly impossible that you should intend to do it, and this is the great reason why so many never actually put Him on.

3. Aim for Action: You must, therefore, not only fully believe that you can, but you must actually intend to put on Christ – to make Him your whole example. Unless it is intended, it will never be done by accident.

4. Make a Sacrifice: You must be fully prepared to make any sacrifice – you must count the cost, and make up your mind to meet the expense necessary to the accomplishment of this end. You must make any sacrifice of friends, property, or credit, which stand in the way.

5. Realize the Importance: You must realize the importance of doing this...persons who do not fully put on the Lord Jesus Christ, while they profess to be His followers, are doing Him, and His cause, the greatest injury of which they are capable. They should then realize the infinite importance of fully representing Him.

6. Pray without Ceasing: Keep up a constant intercourse with Him. You must commune with Him in prayer without ceasing... there must be constant communion with the Spirit of Christ, in order to put Him on and act just as He would.

7. Repent of Sins: You must not rest while there is any unrepented, unconfessed sin between your soul and Him. You must keep a clear medium. If [a Christian] has grieved Christ, and injured His tender feelings, he can have no farther communion with Him, until he has repented, and confessed his faults, and the tender breathings of mutual love are again restored.

8. Stop Self-Reliance: You must cease from all self-dependence. So long as you depend on yourself, you will see no need of putting on Christ.

9. Partake of His Nature: You must avail yourself of His exceeding great and precious promises. You must realize what the promises were given for; and that they were given for you personally. The Apostle Peter says, "Whereby are given unto us, exceeding great and precious promises, that, by these we might be partakers of the divine nature; having escaped the corruption that is in the world through lust." The design of the promises, then, is, to beget in us a universal likeness to the Lord Jesus Christ.

THE CLOAK OF ZEAL

Once you've put on the armor of God – and once you've clothed yourself with the Anointed One – there's yet one more piece of armor you need. It's seldom mentioned in spiritual warfare circles and yet I believe it is the most vital element of our battle garb. You might call it the secret weapon against the enemy, yet it's no secret at all. It's plainly recorded in the Bible. It is the cloak of zeal.

Isaiah prophesied about a time when the Lord saw there was no man to intercede for the oppressed. So He Himself stepped in to save them with His strong arm, and His righteousness sustained Him. Look at what happened next:

> For he put on righteousness as a breastplate, and an helmet of salvation upon his head; and he put on the garments of vengeance for clothing, and was clad with zeal as a cloak.
>
> Isaiah 59:17

You see here that the Lord did not forsake to prepare for war by putting on His breastplate of righteousness, nor did He forget to take the helmet of salvation as He headed into confrontation. But He didn't stop there. He was clad with zeal as a cloak. The NIV version says he "wrapped Himself in zeal as in a cloak." The NASB says He "wrapped Himself with zeal as a mantle." The Message says He "threw a cloak of Passion across His shoulders." The New Living Translation says He, "wrapped Himself in a cloak of divine passion."

ZEAL: YOUR SECRET WEAPON

Can you see it? The Lord Himself does not come on to the scene to deliver the oppressed – to confront wickedness – without wrapping Himself in a cloak of zeal. This is the same divine passion we must take with us into battle as we defend His Word and His honor in the earth. When we wrap ourselves in a cloak of zeal, it's the difference-maker on the battlefield. Zeal can make up for inexperience. Zeal can overcome the spirit of weariness. Zeal is the secret weapon. It's the fire of God that consumes the circumstances that are waging war against your life and God's purposes for you and others. Don't go into battle without zeal.

Keep in mind that prayer is one of the primary weapons of your warfare. The Apostle James reminded us that effective fervent prayers make tremendous power available – God's power (James 5:16). It was Elijah's prayer that brought down fire from heaven, and there was nothing special about Elijah except the anointing. Elijah was a man anointed. If you are born again, that same anointing abides in you. It's the zeal, the fervency, the passion that causes it to rise from within you and affect your circumstances as you release your prayers.

The Apostle Paul said it this way:

> For though we walk in the flesh, we do not war after the flesh: (For the weapons of our warfare are not carnal, but mighty through God to the pulling down of strong holds;) Casting down imaginations, and every high thing that exalteth itself against the knowledge of God, and bringing into captivity every thought to the obedience of Christ; And having in a readiness to revenge all disobedience, when your obedience is fulfilled.

2 Corinthians 10:3-6

The weapons of our warfare aren't machetes and machine guns. Our weapons involve the Word of God and prayer. The Apostle Paul, after he described the armor of God, told us what to do in battle: "Praying always with all prayer and supplication in the Spirit, and watching thereunto with all perseverance and supplication for all saints…" (Ephesians 6:18).

When you go into battle, imitate your God: "The Lord will march out like a mighty man, like a warrior he will stir up his zeal; with a shout he will raise the battle cry and will triumph over his enemies" (Isaiah 42:13 NIV).

Remember this: It's the zeal, this fervency, this passion that puts the umph in the rest of our spiritual armor. All other things being equal, it's the fervency that puts you over. Take two tennis players with the same skill sets. You can give one brand new sneakers, the best racket, some fresh balls, and a special coach. But if he doesn't have passion, then someone with worn out racket, some beat up Converse – and a fervent spirit – will beat his Adidas shorts off.

In our Christian walk, I'd rather have someone on my side who wasn't as seasoned in the things of the Spirit, but has a fervent spirit that refuses to give up, than someone who knows the Word upside down and backwards but is lukewarm on the battlefield. And guess what? So would God. The good news is, God's zeal is nearer than you might think.

A PASSION THAT DOMINATES LIFE

John H. Jowett was born in Halifax, England in 1864. He worked with men of God like D.L. Moody. His life could be characterized by a noble quote: "I have had but one passion, and I have lived for it – the absorbingly arduous yet glorious work of proclaiming the grace and love of our Lord and Savior Jesus Christ." Brother Jowett left us many sermons and, in fact, books of sermons.

One of his last sermons was preached about a year before he went home to be with the Lord in 1923. It was about spiritual fervency. I have included an excerpt from it in this chapter because Brother Jowett explains the notion of spiritual fervor as a defense against the devil far better than I ever could.

So imagine yourself for just a moment sitting in Westminster Congregational Church in London. The year is 1921. The topic is "The Spiritual Glow." The Scripture text is Romans 12:11, "Be fervent in spirit." Let's listen in:

> I want to consider the defensive power of a noble enthusiasm. What do I mean by an enthusiasm? I mean an intense and generous passion for some supreme interest, so passionate that it dominates the life. And what do I mean by the defensive powers of such an enthusiasm? I mean that such a passion gathers all the forces of life into its own swift goings, so that nothing is left to loiter, nothing is left to trail along in aimless vagrancy. Every power is caught in the commanding suction of a great enthusiasm; it is not trapped by any insidious enticement which may be lurking by the way. A noble enthusiasm is defensive because it makes life whole and wholesome. This kind of fire tends to keep everything clean.
>
> Turn where you please you may watch the protective influence of a great enthusiasm. Take a young fellow who

goes to one of our national universities. What does he find? He finds pernicious influences of many kinds. There are germs of enervation which would reduce him to mental lassitude. There are soft enticements which would lull him into moral laxity. But give him a passion for learning, and all these small invaders are burnt up in the fervent heat. A bewitching pleasure, a luring indolence, a seductive mischief – his enthusiasm destroys them as in a consuming fire. The assailments shrivel like moths in a flame. His passion is his defense.

So it is with the reign of any predominant enthusiasm. It has protective ministry. Give a working man a passion for gardening and put him into a garden plot, and what defensive forces his enthusiasm throws round about his leisure hours! All the meaner enticements lose their power. They never reach his central consciousness. Indeed, there is no consciousness to spare. His enthusiasm commands all his forces, and the baser things call to him in vain. His fire is his defense.

WHEN THE FIRE WANES

Although Jesus expects His disciples to deny self, pick up their cross and follow Him, His sermons and illustrations often appealed to self in the sense that

He spelled out the personal benefits of obedience (Matthew 16:24).

For example, Jesus said "Judge not, that ye not be judged" (Matthew 7:1). The fear of being judged may cause some not to be judgmental until they grow enough in the Lord that their character is colored with mercy instead of judgment. Jesus also said to forgive others so your heavenly Father can forgive you, and if you don't forgive others then God won't forgive you (Luke 11:14-15). Jesus is clearly spelling out the benefits of obedience and the consequences of disobedience.

Brother Jowett took a page out of Jesus' stylebook when he offered the flip side of spiritual fervency. The personal benefits of maintaining a fervent spirit – of staying on fire for God – are clear. But so are the consequences for becoming lukewarm. Jesus Himself said He would spew lukewarm believers out of His mouth. The Message Bible puts it this way: "I know you inside and out, and find little to my liking. You're not cold, you're not hot—far better to be either cold or hot! You're stale. You're stagnant. You make me want to vomit" (Revelation 15-16).

Let's listen in once again to Brother Jowett's sermon to get the other side of the story:

> But, when enthusiasm begins to cool, our defensive energy begins to wane. As the fire dies out the enemy comes in. Just as soon as radiation ceases invasion begins.

Mean things appear, and they appear in aggressive pride. It is as when the temperature of the blood is reduced. Waiting plague and lurking disease find entry and foothold and they begin to thrive in the defenseless roads of the flesh.

Admiral Peary has told us, in his account of the discovery of the North Pole, that it was in the dreary, weary Arctic winter, when enthusiasm waned, that the hidden weaknesses of his men appeared. It was then that the spirit of irritation and dissension would breathe disturbing air upon the fellowship.

As the fires died low quarrelsomeness stole in. The moral defenses departed with the glow. And so it is in every relationship of life. When noble fires are burning our estates are secure. When the noble fires smolder our estates are invaded, and mean and baser things possess our spiritual world.

THE GLOW OF CHRIST

Our passion for God must consume us. When we have a fervent spirit, we will not fall into temptation. We will not be distracted by the world. We will walk in His will and in His presence. Your fervency is a hedge of protection, a wall of fire that protects you from the wiles of the enemy.

But sometimes after we get our breakthrough, we lose our fervency. All the things we did to get the breakthrough – the prayer, the fasting, the praising, the confessing, the thanking – we let up when we get the breakthrough. And that's when the enemy comes in to try to steal it away from us. Brother Jowett expounds:

> Now, what is to save us? Nothing but the spiritual glow. We can repel and destroy these emerging evils by feeding the fires of a large and noble enthusiasm. Everybody can help in making the fire. Everybody can bring fuel to the holy flame. We can strengthen it with knowledge, we can feed it with thought, we can quicken it with expression, we can deepen it with prayer. We can live and labor for the passion of fraternity, the enthusiasm of humanity, the glow of Christ, the fire of God.
>
> Our resource, in all our imminent problems, and in all the difficulties which confront us, is to be found in the maintenance of the spiritual glow. I see no hope for the world except in common and enthusiastic devotion to our Lord Jesus Christ. And by devotion to Christ I mean something loftier than ecclesiastical

passion, and something far nobler than denominational pride. I mean that vital, personal, quickening relationship to the Savior which fills the mind and heart with generous and cleansing passion. I mean the spiritual devotion which makes a life conspicuous for magnanimity, chivalry, fraternity, humanity. That fire of God can cleanse the world!

CHAPTER 3
The Fervent Prophet

Then the fire of the Lord fell, and consumed the burnt sacrifice, and the wood, and the stones, and the dust, and licked up the water that was in the trench. And when all the people saw it, they fell on their faces: and they said, The Lord, he is the God; the Lord, he is the God.

1 Kings 18:38

Elijah had a fervent spirit. He was zealous for God. The very name Elijah means "God is Jehovah." Elijah came on the scene in the midst of King Ahab's wicked reign. At his word, fire fell from heaven and rain from the sky.

We don't know much about Elijah's background, other than he was a Tishbite from Gilead. According to tradition, Tishbe was located eight miles from the

Jabbok River, which connects to the Jordan Elijah struck with his mantle so the waters would spread before his crossing. What I'm getting at is this: Elijah wasn't trained in the best seminary. He didn't have any TV preachers to model his ministry after. There weren't any books like this one to teach him what God's word said on any given subject.

Like John the Baptist, when Elijah emerged from the wilderness he was a relative nobody – but all of Israel would soon know his name. Elijah was a compassionate miracle-worker. He was a reformer. But at his core, he really wasn't any different than you or me. The Bible says "Elijah was a human being with a nature such as we have [with feelings, affections, and a constitution like ours]..." (James 5:17). The difference between Elijah and many of us today is his fervent spirit. The Bible says Elijah prayed earnestly, and he has become an example of how to get prayer answers (James 5:16).

FERVENT REFORMATION

Israel was in bad spiritual shape during Ahab's reign. The Bible says Ahab did more to provoke the Lord than any king before him by building altars to Baal and Asherah (1 Kings 17:33). Ahab tried to blame Israel's trouble on Elijah, but the prophet saw the root of the issue and sought to reform the land for the sake of the Lord – and the sake of His people.

You know the scene. Elijah makes a proposition to Ahab. "Summon the people from all over Israel to meet me on Mount Carmel," Elijah said. "And bring the 450 prophets of Baal and the four hundred prophets of Asherah, who eat at Jezebel's table."

Ahab took Elijah up on the offer. He probably figured it was a fixed fight. With 850 well-fed men against a solitary Tishbite, Elijah didn't seem to stand a chance of escaping the fate of the many prophets who fell to the spirit of Jezebel. But a fervent spirit for God defeats a Jezebel spirit all day long. Let's recount the historical event:

> And Elijah came unto all the people, and said, How long halt ye between two opinions? if the Lord be God, follow him: but if Baal, then follow him. And the people answered him not a word.
>
> 1 Kings 18:21-29

The people of Israel were drowning in their own apathy. They wouldn't dedicate themselves to Jehovah, but they weren't completely dedicated to the false God's either. It reminds me of some Latin American countries where the people mix several religions to form a spiritual stew. They add a little bit of Jesus, a little Santeria (an occult religion involving animal sacrifices), a little bit of saint worship, and whatever else happens to fit in the pot. The result is a concoction that stinks in the nostrils of Jehovah God. God expects our full devotion – and He deserve it.

THE WRONG KIND OF FERVENCY

These false prophets demonstrate a profound truth: You can be fervent about the wrong thing. Baal's prophets were fervently worshiping him. They were zealous. They were passionate about their cause. In fact, they were so passionate about their cause they bled for it. Let's take a look:

> Then said Elijah unto the people, I, even I only, remain a prophet of the Lord; but Baal's prophets are four hundred and fifty men.

> Let them therefore give us two bullocks; and let them choose one bullock for themselves, and cut it in pieces, and lay it on wood, and put no fire under: and I will dress the other bullock, and lay it on wood, and put no fire under: And call ye on the name of your gods, and I will call on the name of the Lord: and the God that answereth by fire, let him be God. And all the people answered and said, It is well spoken.

> And Elijah said unto the prophets of Baal, Choose you one bullock for yourselves, and dress it first; for ye are many; and call on the name of your gods, but put no fire under. And they took the bullock which was given them, and they dressed it, and called on the name of Baal from morning even until noon, saying, O

Baal, hear us. But there was no voice, nor any that answered. And they leaped upon the altar which was made.

And it came to pass at noon, that Elijah mocked them, and said, Cry aloud: for he is a god; either he is talking, or he is pursuing, or he is in a journey, or peradventure he sleepeth, and must be awaked. And they cried aloud, and cut themselves after their manner with knives and lancets, till the blood gushed out upon them. And it came to pass, when midday was past, and they prophesied until the time of the offering of the evening sacrifice, that there was neither voice, nor any to answer, nor any that regarded.

1 Kings 18:21-29

How many Christians today do we see who are willing to sacrifice to participate in an evangelistic community outreach for a few hours on Saturday morning? Far too few. Yet these false prophets were willing to bleed for their cause. Of course, it got them nothing but cuts all over their body and sore throats from prophesying all day. No eternal good can come from fervent devotion to idols.

What about you? Are you fervent about the wrong thing? Do you sacrifice your time and money to your idols or to your God? Do you spend every night laying on the couch watching TV when you could devote a little more time to study, prayer or ministering to someone? I'm not suggesting you shouldn't watch TV, but I'm absolutely declaring that if TV has become an idol in your life you need to hold a broadcast fast. Turn it off! Many things can become idols in our lives, family, work, entertainment...let us steer clear of misdirected passions that rob us of a closer relationship with Him.

REBUIDLING THE ALTAR

Now let's look at Elijah's response to this unconstrained idol worship. Let's see how a real prophet responds to the idolatry in the land. Let's look at how a believer with a fervent spirit, zealous for God, moves to defend His honor.

> And Elijah said unto all the people, Come near unto me. And all the people came near unto him. And he repaired the altar of the Lord that was broken down. And Elijah took twelve stones, according to the number of the tribes of the sons of Jacob, unto whom the word of the Lord came, saying, Israel shall be thy name: And with the stones he built an altar in the name of the Lord: and he made a trench about the altar, as great as would contain two measures of seed.

> And he put the wood in order, and cut the bullock in pieces, and laid him on the

wood, and said, Fill four barrels with water, and pour it on the burnt sacrifice, and on the wood. And he said, Do it the second time. And they did it the second time. And he said, Do it the third time. And they did it the third time. And the water ran round about the altar; and he filled the trench also with water.

1 Kings 18:30-35

Praise God! Elijah didn't leave any room for anyone to question whether or not his wood was wet and his God was real. He set the stage for a mighty miracle. But there's another lesson in this passage. It doesn't matter how much water the enemy throws on somebody who's fervent in spirit. Circumstances can't waterlog an on-fire believer. If you are truly fervent, the fire of God in your belly will keep burning no matter what the enemy pours on or how thick he pours it. It may even look like life's got you down for the count, completely drenched with trouble, but God's fire will break through, consume those circumstances, and energize you for the next showdown. Hallelujah!

STANDING IN YOUR CALLING

Now, something interesting happens in this next verse. You remember that I wrote of Elijah coming from the land of Tishbe.

> And it came to pass at the time of the
> offering of the evening sacrifice, that
> Elijah the prophet came near...

> 1 Kings 18:36

Not Elijah the Tishbite, Elijah the prophet. Not Brother Elijah, Elijah the prophet. Elijah was standing in his God-given office, fervent in spirit, rebuilding the altars, turning the hearts of men back to the Father, refusing to compromise even though he was far outnumbered by the enemy.

ELIJAH'S FERVENT HEART

Here we see Elijah's motive laid bear, his mouth speaking from the abundance of his heart, his effectual fervent prayer. Elijah wasn't trying to look super-spiritual like some prophets you see praying in the church today. Elijah wasn't trying to show the onlookers how connected he was with the King of glory. No, he was seeking to defend God's honor. He was determined to expose the enemy and deliver the people from bondage.

> Elijah the prophet came near, and said,
> Lord God of Abraham, Isaac, and of
> Israel, let it be known this day that thou
> art God in Israel, and that I am thy
> servant, and that I have done all these
> things at thy word. Hear me, O Lord,
> hear me, that this people may know that

thou art the Lord God, and that thou
hast turned their heart back again.

1 Kings 18:36

God heard Elijah's effectual, fervent prayer. God
listened to the cries of His servant. God responded to
the pure motives of Elijah's heart, which was beating
in rhythm with His.

> Then the fire of the Lord fell, and
> consumed the burnt sacrifice, and the
> wood, and the stones, and the dust, and
> licked up the water that was in the
> trench. And when all the people saw it,
> they fell on their faces: and they said, The
> Lord, he is the God; the Lord, he is the
> God. And Elijah said unto them, Take
> the prophets of Baal; let not one of them
> escape. And they took them: and Elijah
> brought them down to the brook
> Kishon, and slew them there.

1 Kings 18:37-40

This was a great victory – a major breakthrough. We
saw people delivered from the deception of the
enemy. We saw a nation beginning to turn back
toward God. And then we saw the retaliation after he
got his breakthrough. Yes, I said retaliation. That's
why you need to maintain a fervent spirit. Remember,
the fervent spirit is your defense against the devil.

CHAPTER 4
When the Enemy Attacks

When the devil had finished all this tempting, he left him until an opportune time.

Luke 4:13

As the dust settles on the battlefield, there are two things that are certain: the enemy will wait for an opportune time to retaliate and your victory in Christ is assured. It's important for you to remember those two things.

After Satan finished tempting Jesus in the wilderness – trying to get Him to use His authority the wrong way, trying to get Him to sell out for the glory of worldly kingdoms, and trying to get Him to act based on a perversion of Scripture – the Bible says Satan left. But it also says he was laying in wait for another opportunity (Luke 4:13).

The devil is always laying in wait for an opportunity to strike, and sometimes there's no better time than after a great victory. That's because after a great victory we tend to do one of two things (or both). We tend to go into celebration mode or we are so exhausted from the battle that we hunker down in our caves and wait for a refreshing.

When we go into celebration mode, sometimes we strip off the heavy armor God supplies and dance wildly before the Lord in praise. That's wonderful. But just know that while you are dancing with wild abandon the devil is looking upon you like Michal looked at David as he danced alongside the ark of the Lord as it returned to Israel: The devil will despise you in his heart. And the devil is actively making plans for retaliation.

On the other hand, when we go into exhaustion mode, we feel too weak to carry around the heavy armor God supplies, so we lay it aside to get some rest. Times of refreshing are certainly appropriate, and you should have seasons of spiritual reprieve. Although we are in a war for the souls of mankind, we should have some God-given reprieve from our individual battles from time to time. But we need to be wise, knowing what the will of the Lord is. To everything there is a season and a time to every purpose under heaven; a time of war and a time of peace (Ecclesiastes 3). If you lay down at the wrong time, the devil will take the opportunity to attack.

JEZEBEL'S PROPHETIC RETALIATION

With all this in mind, let's look once again to the Prophet Elijah. He had just won a major victory. He slew 850 false prophets with the edge of the sword. Thousands turned away from idols and back to Jehovah. The result: the drought was over. Elijah told Ahab to celebrate because of the sound of the abundance of rain.

Elijah went to the top of Carmel and prayed an effective fervent prayer until the rain manifested (1 Kings 18:41-46; James 5:16-18). This was another victory for Elijah, who had told Ahab earlier that it would not rain except by his word (1 Kings 17:1). The hand of the Lord was on Elijah and he ran all the way to Jezreel, nearly 20 miles. He outran Ahab's chariot.

Elijah was on a spiritual high. And then it happened. The enemy launched a counter attack. Jezebel released her prophetic retaliation and it sent Elijah into a spiritual tailspin – and it took him weeks to recover. Let's listen in to this fateful moment:

> And Ahab told Jezebel all that Elijah had done, and withal how he had slain all the prophets with the sword.

Then Jezebel sent a messenger unto Elijah, saying, So let the gods do to me, and more also, if I make not thy life as the life of one of them by to morrow about this time.

And when he saw that, he arose, and went for his life, and came to Beersheba, which belongeth to Judah, and left his servant there.

1 Kings 19:1-3

Stop right there. The Bible says, "When he saw that…" Not when he heard it, but when he saw it. Jezebel released fearful imaginations at Elijah via a messenger. And the Bible says Elijah "saw it." Of course, Elijah was a prophet and his spiritual eyes were sensitive to the realm of the spirit. He was probably used to having dreams and visions. But what he saw – Jezebel's threat against his life becoming a stark reality – wasn't God showing Elijah a vision. It was a fearful imagination in his soul.

IMAGINATIONS RUNNING WILD

It's too bad the Apostle Paul wasn't there to exhort Elijah to cast down the imagination and the high and lofty threat that exalted itself against the knowledge of God. Elijah was blessed, not cursed, the head and not the tail, above only and not beneath (Deuteronomy 28). Elijah had God-given spiritual authority in the earth. All Jezebel had, by contrast, was the authority she usurped from her wicked husband, the false gods she served, and the false prophets she fed.

But Elijah took the bait. His imagination ran wild and, moments after two magnanimous breakthroughs, Elijah was on the run again. This time, it wasn't by the leading of the Holy Ghost. It was by the leading of the spirit of fear. And that fear led him out of the will of God, perhaps for the first time in his service to the Lord.

The spirit of fear is a common tactic post-breakthrough. Its goal is to steal your breakthrough by convincing you that it won't last, or that you didn't really get a breakthrough in the first place. When people get healed, the devil often tries to bring back the same old symptoms, along with fearful suggestions that the disease really didn't go.

When we accept those suggestions – retaliation for the victory – we invite the devil to put the disease back on us. The same goes for any breakthrough. If the devil can use fear, doubt, or some circumstantial evidence to rob out victory, he'll do it. He works with figurative smoke and mirrors. But when we stay fervent in spirit, we'll catch his attempts to deceive us, weary us, and otherwise scare us out of God's will. Thank God, we can always repent and get back on track.

A PROPHETIC SOAP OPERA

It took Elijah some weeks to get back on track after his run in with Jezebel. He journeyed down into the self-pity pit and wallowed around there. This is what I like to call prophetic soap opera. It seems some prophets have a tendency to get melancholy and even dramatic. Elijah and Jonah are two prophets that come to mind. Let's listen in to Elijah's unfolding soap opera.

> But [Elijah] himself went a day's journey into the wilderness, and came and sat down under a juniper tree: and he requested for himself that he might die; and said, It is enough; now, O Lord, take away my life; for I am not better than my fathers.
>
> 1 Kings 19:3-4

Oh, dear! Sounds sort of like Jonah sitting under the gourd, doesn't it? Have you ever been in a place where you said, "God, just take me on to heaven now? I can't deal with this anymore?" I'll admit that I have. If God was listening (later, I always hope he wasn't) he didn't even dignify my whining with an answer.

Elijah wanted to die right then and there – or so he said. If he really wanted to die he wouldn't have ran from Jezebel. The point is this: What happened to his fervent spirit? He took his focus of God and put it on himself. He fell into the trap of self-pity. He felt lonely. God is so merciful, though, that He gave Elijah some time to gather himself.

And as he lay and slept under a juniper tree, behold, then an angel touched him, and said unto him, Arise and eat.

And he looked, and, behold, there was a cake baken on the coals, and a cruse of water at his head. And he did eat and drink, and laid him down again.

And the angel of the Lord came again the second time, and touched him, and said, Arise and eat; because the journey is too great for thee.

And he arose, and did eat and drink, and went in the strength of that meat forty days and forty nights unto Horeb the mount of God.

And he came thither unto a cave, and lodged there; and, behold, the word of the Lord came to him, and he said unto him, What doest thou here, Elijah?

1 Kings 19:5-9

God called Elijah out. He had work for Elijah to do and he needed His servant to get on with it. But at this point, Elijah had exchanged his fervent spirit for self-pity. You can hear it in the prophet's response to God's question:

And he said, I have been very jealous for
the Lord God of hosts: for the children
of Israel have forsaken thy covenant,
thrown down thine altars, and slain thy
prophets with the sword; and I, even I
only, am left; and they seek my life, to
take it away.

1 Kings 19:5-10

Um... did Elijah forget what just happened? The
Israelites had witnessed the glory of God, turned their
hearts back to Him, and helped capture the prophets
of Baal and Jezebel so Elijah could cleanse the land of
these wicked idolaters. But Elijah was still thinking
about Jezebel's threat on his life. God tried to snap
Elijah out of his Jezebel-induced funk.

And he said, Go forth, and stand upon
the mount before the Lord. And, behold,
the Lord passed by, and a great and
strong wind rent the mountains, and
brake in pieces the rocks before the
Lord; but the Lord was not in the wind:
and after the wind an earthquake; but the
Lord was not in the earthquake: And
after the earthquake a fire; but the Lord
was not in the fire: and after the fire a
still small voice.

And it was so, when Elijah heard it, that he wrapped his face in his mantle, and went out, and stood in the entering in of the cave.

1 Kings 19:11-13

Elijah wrapped his face in his mantle. That statement struck me because this is the same mantle that he used to part the waters. The same mantle he used to call Elisha into ministry. Why did Elijah wrap his face in his mantle? I believe it was a sign of Elijah's humility before the Lord. The wind didn't move him. The earthquake didn't move him. The fire didn't move him. But when Elijah heard the still, small voice of the Lord he responded immediately.

And, behold, there came a voice unto him, and said, What doest thou here, Elijah?

And he said, I have been very jealous for the Lord God of hosts: because the children of Israel have forsaken thy covenant, thrown down thine altars, and slain thy prophets with the sword; and I, even I only, am left; and they seek my life, to take it away.

1 Kings 19:13-14

Elijah was still telling the same old story. At this point, God knew He needed to get Elijah focused on His work instead of his 'self.' God also knew Elijah needed some relationships in his life. His servant never did return to his side. Elijah needed to hook up with some others who were fervent in spirit, like Jehu and Elisha. So God told Elijah to go and anoint them and Elijah rose again to fulfill his calling. God motivated Elijah with a glimpse of what was about to happen, and also let Elijah know he wasn't alone. Praise the Lord!

JONAH VERSUS ELIJAH

Elijah stumbled, fell, but rose again to fulfill his calling. The Bible says a righteous man falls seven times, but he gets back up again (Proverbs 24:16). And therein lies the difference between Jonah and Elijah. Elijah was righteous. Jonah was self-righteous. You can't be self-righteous and truly zealous for God at the same time. If you are self-righteous, you are zealous for your self.

So why did Jonah stay rebellious while Elijah stayed obedient? I submit to you it was because of Elijah's fervency for the Lord. Elijah was fervent in spirit. When the attack came, he stumbled, but he got back up again. Jonah, meanwhile, stumbled over his own judgmental, self-righteous attitude. I write more about this prophetic pitfall in my book, "The Heart of the Prophetic: Keys to flowing in a more powerful prophetic anointing."

On the one hand we have Jonah, whose last known action in the Bible was sitting under a gourd, so angry he wished he was dead because God showed mercy on Nineveh (Jonah 4:9). On the other hand you have Elijah who was taken to heaven in grand style after serving the Lord with a fervent spirit. Then still on the other hand you have Elijah's servant, Elisha's predecessor.

ELIJAH'S OTHER SERVANT

I want to stop right here and take you on a little bunny trail, if that's alright. I want to, for a moment, explore Elijah's servant. Elijah was running for his life. His servant was supposed to protect him. Instead, he stayed behind in Beersheba. Elijah could have used some support. He didn't need to be isolated in the wilderness with his fearful imaginations of Jezebel's henchman catching up with him. But there's no indication that Elijah's servant even so much as tried to stand by his side.

That has always puzzled me. Elijah's servant had just watched God bring rain to the land at Elijah's word after a long drought. Elijah's servant had just witnessed Elijah call down fire from heaven. Elijah's servant had witnessed his man of God defeat 850 prophets with his sword. God only knows how many other miracles Elijah's servant witnessed. Yet at the first sign of trouble, Elijah's servant failed to discern his need and stayed behind in Beersheba, a fertile land of plenty, while Elijah isolated himself in the wilderness.

Well, Elijah's servant missed out. That's the last we hear of Elijah's servant. He could have been in line for a double portion anointing, but he forfeited it by not sticking with Elijah through thick and thin. God gave Elijah a new servant not too long after this. God gave him Elisha to carry on his ministry. In contrast to Elijah's first servant, Elisha refused to leave his side. Elijah even commanded him twice to stay behind and Elisha refused to heave him.

From the beginning, you can see Elisha's fervent spirit for the Lord. Elisha was plowing with 12 yoke of oxen when Elijah passed by him and cast his mantle upon him. Let's listen in to the chronicle:

And he left the oxen, and ran after Elijah, and said, Let me, I pray thee, kiss my father and my mother, and then I will follow thee. And he said unto him, Go back again: for what have I done to thee?

And he returned back from him, and took a yoke of oxen, and slew them, and boiled their flesh with the instruments of the oxen, and gave unto the people, and they did eat. Then he arose, and went after Elijah, and ministered unto him.

1 Kings 19:19-21

Elisha served Elijah faithfully – and fervently. He was widely known in the Kingdom of Israel as the one who poured water over Elijah's hands (1 Kings 3:11). Through his faithful, fervent service to Elijah, Elisha was actually serving God's purposes in the earth and being prepared to do even greater works than Elijah.

But when Elijah's time was drawing to an end, would Elisha stick with him or rush out to launch his own ministry before God's perfect timing? Would Elisha hang tough with Elijah no matter where he went or what he did? Or would he take any excuse to bail out when the warfare got intense like Elijah's other servant did when Jezebel came calling? Elijah gave his apprentice three chances to leave his service.

It reminds me of when Jesus asked Peter, "Do you love me?" three times. Jesus was giving Peter more responsibility for the church in that process. Elisha may or may not have known it, but Elijah was about to give him a great responsibility – as his successor. Elisha had already been anointed as his successor, but now it was nearing time to take the mantle of responsibility and carry on where Elijah would leave off (1 Kings 19:15-16). Let's look at Elisha's trio of tests:

> Just before God took Elijah to heaven in a whirlwind, Elijah and Elisha were on a walk out of Gilgal. Elijah said to Elisha, "Stay here. God has sent me on an errand to Bethel."

Elisha said, "Not on your life! I'm not letting you out of my sight!" So they both went to Bethel.

The guild of prophets at Bethel met Elisha and said, "Did you know that God is going to take your master away from you today?"

"Yes," he said, "I know it. But keep it quiet."

Then Elijah said to Elisha, "Stay here. God has sent me on an errand to Jericho."

Elisha said, "Not on your life! I'm not letting you out of my sight!" So they both went to Jericho.

The guild of prophets at Jericho came to Elisha and said, "Did you know that God is going to take your master away from you today?"

"Yes," he said, "I know it. But keep it quiet."

Then Elijah said to Elisha, "Stay here. God has sent me on an errand to the Jordan."

Elisha said, "Not on your life! I'm not letting you out of my sight!" And so the two of them went their way together.

2 Kings 2:1-6 (Message)

Elisha knew his master was about to go up to heaven. Instead of bailing on him, he stuck closely by Elijah's side to draw everything he could from him.

And it came to pass, when they were gone over, that Elijah said unto Elisha, Ask what I shall do for thee, before I be taken away from thee. And Elisha said, I pray thee, let a double portion of thy spirit be upon me. And he said, Thou hast asked a hard thing: nevertheless, if thou see me when I am taken from thee, it shall be so unto thee; but if not, it shall not be so.

2 Kings 2:8-10

Elisha was bold enough to ask Elijah for a double portion of his anointing before he went on to be with the Lord. He knew he would need it to continue the work of the ministry. Based on his service up to that time, Elijah was willing to entertain the request. But would Elisha stick by his side until the end? Elisha would have to if he wanted that double portion.

And it came to pass as they went on, and talked…"

2 Kings 2:11

I like that. They walked on together and they talked. Can you imagine what they were talking about? Both men knew that their time together was limited. This was Elisha's last chance to draw wisdom from his mentor. Elijah's last chance to offer his spiritual son instruction. And while they were talking, a chariot of fire parted them and Elijah went up by a whirlwind into the heavens.

And Elisha saw it. And Elisha received the double portion anointing for which he petitioned. And here's my point: Elijah's other servant, the one who stayed behind at Beersheba, was a candidate for this double portion anointing. At the very least, he was in line to receive a mighty impartation from Elijah.

But Elijah's other servant wasn't willing to go with him through the hard times, to the hard places, with the hard words. Elijah's other servant didn't have a fervent spirit, serving the Lord. So Elijah's other servant disappears into Bible obscurity, without even so much as a name by which to call him. But the Bible says Elisha went on to do twice as many miracles as his mentor. Elisha maintained his fervency until the end. Elisha was so fervent in spirit that the miraculous followed him after he was dead and buried.

And it came to pass, as they were burying a man, that, behold, they spied a band of men; and they cast the man into the sepulchre of Elisha: and when the man was let down, and touched the bones of Elisha, he revived, and stood up on his feet.

2 Kings 2:11

CHAPTER 5
Are You *Really* on Fire?

Jesus gave Himself for us that He might redeem us from every lawless deed and purify for Himself His own special people, zealous for good works.

Titus 2:14

So I'll ask you the question again…Are you on fire for God? Maybe it would help if we outlined the characteristics of a fervent spirit. Ask yourself the questions below and be honest. It's just you and God and He already knows every single solitary one of your weaknesses. Even if you are a little lukewarm, He still loves you. This is your chance to look into the mirror of the Word, see the truth, and, if necessary, take steps to rekindle your fire.

1. Are you eager to serve the Lord?

The Bible says we were created in Christ for good works, which God prepared beforehand that we should walk in them (Ephesians 2:10). The Bible also says "Jesus gave Himself for us that He might redeem us from every lawless deed and purify for Himself His own special people, zealous for good works" (Titus 2:14).

If you aren't marked by fervent partisanship for Christ and His cause, then you aren't on fire for God. The Bible says faith, if it does not have works (deeds and actions of obedience to back it up), by itself is destitute of power (inoperative, dead) (James 2:17). You can tell everyone you meet how much you love the Lord. You can worship until your voice gives out. You can work up a sweat cutting a rug in church during your favorite praise song. But that doesn't prove you are on fire for God.

Again, Jesus gave Himself for us that He might redeem us from every lawless deed and purify for Himself His own special people, zealous for good works (Titus 2:14). We are supposed to be zealous for good works. When your pastor asks you to serve in the church, you should not be slothful in business, but fervent in spirit, serving the Lord (Romans 12:11).

Maybe you got offended because Sister So and So was asked to sing a solo and you weren't even allowed to be in the choir. Maybe you were hurt because Brother So and So was selected to head the men's ministry and you were asked to help paint the church. But the Bible clearly states:

> Whatever may be your task, work at it heartily (from the soul), as [something done] for the Lord and not for men, Knowing [with all certainty] that it is from the Lord [and not from men] that you will receive the inheritance which is your [real] reward. [The One Whom] you are actually serving [is] the Lord Christ (the Messiah).
>
> Colossians 3:24-25 (AMP)

What about at the workplace? Are you doing everything there as unto the Lord? What about the homefront? Wherever we find ourselves, we need to represent Christ by engaging wholeheartedly in the task at hand. If we truly do everything as unto the Lord, our motives will stay pure and God's blessings will flow. If we have any other motives, our works won't stand up on Judgment Day.

> Every man's work shall be made manifest: for the day shall declare it, because it shall be revealed by fire; and the fire shall try every man's work of what sort it is. If any man's work abide which he hath built thereupon, he shall receive a reward. If any man's work shall

be burned, he shall suffer loss: but he himself shall be saved; yet so as by fire.

1 Corinthians 3:13-15

Let me put it to you this way. If your works are motivated by a fiery passion for God, the fire won't burn them up. Your work will abide and you will receive a reward. Stir up your zeal and stay focused on why you are doing what you are doing. When you do, you'll experience supernatural grace that makes the job so much easier.

2. What is the motivation of your heart?

Again, when we do things as unto the Lord, the Lord rewards us. It's part of seeking His righteousness, or His right causes. When we do things to be seen of men, to attain a certain position, status or title, our motivation is wrong. Not only are we slothful in the Lord's business, we are downright religious. Jesus warned,

> Take heed that ye do not your alms before men, to be seen of them: otherwise ye have no reward of your Father which is in heaven. Therefore, when thou doest thine alms, do not sound a trumpet before thee, as the hypocrites do in the synagogues and in the streets, that they may have glory of men. Verily I say unto you, they have their rewards. But when thou doest alms,

let not thy left hand know what they right hand doeth: That thine alms may be in secret: and they Father which seeth in secret himself shall reward you openly" (Matthew 6:1-6).

Jesus was describing a religious spirit. Jesus was dealing with the heart of man. These people were hypocrites because a zeal for God wasn't their motivation for helping. They saw the world as their stage – and they sought the praises of men. When our motivation is not a passion for God and a love for man, we are engaging in dead works.

Before we move on, let's look at how the Message Bible translates Matthew 6:1-6. I think it drives home the point in modern language we can all appreciate. If Jesus was here today, is it possible He'd say it something like this?:

Be especially careful when you are trying to be good so that you don't make a performance out of it. It might be good theater, but the God who made you won't be applauding. When you do something for someone else, don't call attention to yourself. You've seen them in action, I'm sure—'playactors' I call them—treating prayer meeting and street corner alike as a stage, acting compassionate as long as someone is watching, playing to the crowds. They get applause, true, but that's all they get. When you help someone out, don't think about how it looks. Just do it—quietly and unobtrusively. That is the way your God, who conceived you in love, working behind the scenes, helps you out.

3. Are you diligent to complete the work you started?

Many of us start on a God-given project with zeal, but do we finish it with the same fervent spirit? It's important to maintain a fervent spirit from beginning to end. Sure, at the beginning of some new and exciting endeavor you've got emotions on your side. But you can't depend on those emotions to carry you to the finish line. You need a fervent spirit to remain diligent in the face of opposition.

When the Apostle Paul told the Romans not to be slothful in business, he was warning against apathy. A sloth is someone who is not inclined to work, who is spiritually apathetic or inactive. A sloth is lethargic. Slothfulness and diligence aren't compatible but diligence and a fervent spirit run hand in hand.

Scottish Theologian William Barclay, who dedicated his life to making the best biblical scholarship available to the average reader and compiled the Daily Study Bible, put it this way: "There is a certain intensity in the Christian life. There is no room for lethargy in it."

Old Testament prophets warned against having a slothful spirit. Amos pronounced woe upon those who were at ease in Zion (Amos 6:1). Jeremiah wrote, "Cursed is the one who does the Lord's work negligently. And cursed be the one who restrains his sword from blood" (Jeremiah 48:10 NASB).

God is by no means going to curse us or bring woe to our households if we aren't diligent in His business. But I can confidently tell you that you won't receive the fullness of His blessing and you won't fulfill His call on your life if you are slothful in His business. Consider what the Holy Spirit wrote in the Book of Hebrews:

> God is not unjust; he will not forget your work and the love you have shown him as you have helped his people and continue to help them. We want each of you to show this same diligence to the very end, in order to make your hope sure. We do not want you to become lazy, but to imitate those who through faith and patience inherit what has been promised.
>
> Hebrews 6:10-12

We will all stand before our Father in heaven one day and give an account of our time here on earth. If you have a habit of slacking off before the end of a project, you aren't really on fire for God. You need to rekindle the flames so you can abound in diligence (2 Corinthians 8:7).

4. Are you committed to God's will, no matter what it is?

If you are on fire for God, you will be zealous to do His will – even if it doesn't seem reasonable to your mind or pleasant to your flesh. Jesus Christ is the best example we have. In the Garden of Gethsemane, Jesus committed Himself to doing the will of the Father, even though it meant beatings, slander, crucifixion and all manner of abuse.

It's normal to want to escape suffering. Nobody normal person likes suffering in and of itself. Even Christ asked the Father to let the cup of crucifixion pass from Him, if it were possible. But He added eight words at the end of that prayer that demonstrated His fervent spirit: "Nevertheless not as I will, but as thou wilt" (Matthew 26:39).

God is not going to ask you to willfully submit to a literal crucifixion for the sin of the world. There need be only one Lamb of God. That job is finished. But He may ask you to willfully submit to a figurative crucifixion of your flesh to put your own sinful behaviors to death. Only you can make the choice to, as Paul put it, "die daily" (1 Corinthians 15:31).

5. Are you faithful?

A fervent spirit is a faithful spirit. Let me say it again. A fervent spirit is a faithful spirit. If you are truly fervent in spirit, you will faithfully serve the Lord whether your aging flesh feels like it or not. You'll be in church when the doors open. You'll be on your post at all times, whatever that post may be. You'll be faithful to study God's Word. In essence, you'll be faithful unto God in all things. Anything else is spiritual adultery.

In the Book of Hosea, God deals with a spirit of harlotry. The spirit of harlotry is a spirit that's unfaithful to God. The Apostle James warned believers to purify their hearts of spiritual adultery (James 4:8 AMP). Our idols lead us into unfaithfulness. When we stay home from church to watch the basketball game, that's idolatry. When God is calling us to study and pray and we go to the mall instead, that's idolatry. Idols don't have any power in and of themselves to woo us into unfaithfulness. Idols only have the power we give them. Are you fervently serving your idols are God?

When you are fervent in spirit, you'll be faithful to the plans, purposes and pursuits of God. God will honor you and promote you along the way. Jesus said, "He that is faithful in that which is least is faithful also in much: and he that is unjust in the least is unjust also in much" (Luke 16:10). A fervent spirit is an insurance policy against spiritual adultery. The Lord promises, "Mine eyes shall be upon the faithful of the land, that they may dwell with me: he that walketh in a perfect way, he shall serve me" (Psalm 101:6).

6. Can you humble yourself for Christ's cause?

Humility is the sign of a fervent spirit. Why? Because humility glorifies Christ. When we humble ourselves in the face of persecution, when we humble ourselves in the face of praise, when we humble ourselves in the face of false accusations – that demonstrates a trust in the Lord as our vindicator. Christ's passion demanded humility. And so must ours.

If we're passionate for Him and His causes, we will not allow pride to manifest when someone mistreats us or when God honors us. We'll exercise the fruit of self-control despite how we feel.

We'll remain meek and lowly of heart like Christ Himself. Christ was so passionate about the souls of mankind that He did some extraordinary things. Read the following verse slowly and consider whether or not you are truly humble:

> Who, being in the form of God, thought it not robbery to be equal with God: But made himself of no reputation, and took upon him the form of a servant, and was made in the likeness of men: And being found in fashion as a man, he humbled himself, and became obedient unto death, even the death of the cross.

Philippians 2:6-8

It's was one thing for Jesus to humble Himself and walk among us. It was another thing for Jesus to make himself of no reputation. It was still another thing for Jesus to humble Himself unto death. But it was an altogether amazing act of love to humble Himself to the death of the cross, which was reserved for the worst criminal elements of His day.

Christ did all of that for you and for me. Can you now humble yourself for His cause? If you have a fervent spirit, humility is a simple walk. A fervent spirit is a humble spirit.

7. Are you obedient?

A fervent spirit is also an obedient spirit. The Lord once said to me, "I am looking for people in this last hour who will listen to My voice and walk in my Word. Will you do this?" My answer, of course, was "yes." I'm sure your answer is "yes" also. Listening to His voice is the exciting part. Sometimes walking in the Word, whether the written Word or a prophetic word, is a little tougher. But it's much easier with a fervent spirit.

The Bible says, "If you are willing and obedient, ye shall eat the good of the land" (Isaiah 1:19). The Lord once told me this, "Willingness is insurance against disobedience." If you are willing, you will obey. If you are not willing, you may obey for a while because you know it is the right thing to do. But you will eventually rebel because your will is not with you. If you have a fervent spirit, you will maintain your obedience. That's what the Lord is looking for.

Samuel once asked a pivotal question that we should all remember the answer to:

> Hath the Lord as great delight in burnt offerings and sacrifices, as in obeying the voice of the Lord? Behold, to obey is better than sacrifice, and to hearken than the fat of rams. For rebellion is as the sin of witchcraft, and stubbornness is as iniquity and idolatry.
>
> 1 Samuel 15:22-25

We are called unto obedience – even in our thought life (2 Corinthians 10:5). We may have to suffer a bit to learn how to obey. I know I did. But that's OK. I'm not embarrassed to admit it because I'm in good company. The Bible says Jesus learned obedience through the things He suffered (Hebrews 5:8). If you have a fervent spirit, you'll suffer less, learn more quickly, and glorify God more.

8. Will you serve another man's vision?

Oftentimes serving the Lord means serving men. In other words, there is some leader in your life that has a vision, a call – and he needs your help. If you are called alongside this leader, then your job is to help forward that vision – with a fervent spirit. Your job is to do the will of God from your heart (Ephesians 6:6). Consider the Message translation of this verse:

> Servants, respectfully obey your earthly masters but always with an eye to obeying the real master, Christ. Don't just do what you have to do to get by, but work heartily, as Christ's servants doing what God wants you to do. And work with a smile on your face, always keeping in mind that no matter who happens to be giving the orders, you're really serving God. Good work will get you good pay from the Master, regardless of whether you are slave or free.

I like that… "Always keeping in mind that no matter who happens to be giving the orders, you're really serving God." There's something in the Church called the "my ministry" syndrome. Folks have a tendency to want to launch their own ministry rather than serve in another. Sometimes it's premature and the ministry buckles under because the person's character couldn't keep them where their anointing took them. But sometimes that person was never called to begin with and the ministry becomes a dead work at best and a disaster at worst.

God may have a ministry prepared for you that is separate and apart from where you are currently serving. But God's timing is vital. Jesus said, "And if ye have not been faithful in that which is another man's, who shall give you that which is your own?" (Luke 16:12). While you are serving another man's vision, do it with a fervent spirit. Wouldn't you expect those God sends you to do the same if it were your vision? You reap what you sow. Even David served Saul for a season, and did so respectfully.

9. What's the temperature of your prayer life?

There have been many books written on prayer and there will probably be many more written. So I don't want to get into what prayer is and what prayer isn't and how to pray and when to pray and how long to pray. If you have a prayer life, you know it. If you don't, you know it too. A person who is fervent in spirit is fervent in prayer.

Paul said we are to be "instant in prayer" (Romans 12:12). He also said we should be "praying always with all prayer and supplication in the Spirit" (Ephesians 6:18). Peter said we should watch unto prayer (1 Peter 4:7). Jesus said to "pray for those who despitefully use you" (Luke 6:28). Paul said to "pray without ceasing" (1 Thessalonians 5:17).

If you need to stir your prayer life up, meditate on God's promises regarding prayer. For example, Jesus said, "All things, whatsoever ye shall ask in prayer, believing, ye shall receive" (Matthew 21:22). He also said, "What things soever ye desire, when ye pray, believe that ye receive them and you shall have them" (Mark 11:24). The effective fervent prayer of a righteous man availeth much (James 5:16).

10. What's your mouth up to?

We'll round out our fervent spirit check up with a look at the mouth. What's coming out of your orifice? Jesus said, "Out of the abundance of the heart the mouth speaks" (Matthew 12:34). Whatever is in your heart in abundance is going to come out of your mouth.

If you are on fire for God, you are going be speaking to yourself in psalms, hymns, and spiritual songs, singing and making melody in your heart to the Lord, giving thanks always for all things unto God and the Father in the name of our Lord Jesus Christ (Ephesians 5:19-20). That's a sign of being filled with the Spirit – and it's a sign of fervency.

Remember, we can't fool God. Jesus knows those who draw near to Him with their mouth and honor Him with their lips but have a heart that is far from Him (Matthew 15:8). The Bible says not to let any corrupt communication proceed from our mouth, but only that which is edifying and ministers grace to the hearers (Ephesians 4:29). If blessing and curses are coming out of the same mouth, you aren't fervent enough.

By contrast, if you are on fire for God He will give you a mouth and wisdom, which your adversaries shall not be able to stand against or refute (Luke 21:15). Do you want to have a voice in the earth today? Then sell out to God and stay on fire for His plans and He'll use you to speak wisdom into the earth.

CHAPTER 6
Repent, Refresh, Refire

*Repent ye therefore, and turn again, that your sins may be
blotted out, that so there may come seasons of refreshing from the
presence of the Lord...*

Acts 3:19 (ASV)

Repentance. When you think of that word you may
think of tear-stained pews in your local Holiness
church. Or you may think of some time when you
were wallowing in sorrow over a mistake you made
that hurt the Lord. Or perhaps you think of David as
he wrote the 51st Psalm.

The word repentance stirs different images – and
different feelings – in different people. It's time to
make sure we have a biblical perspective of
repentance and not just the perspective we learned in

Sunday School when we were six years old. True repentance is something to be valued, something to be sought after, and something to receive.

If you read this far in the book, you should have a pretty good idea whether you are on fire for God or not. If not, you need to repent. God expects fervency. That's the plain and simple truth. But before you launch into repentance as you see it, let's take the time to learn more about repentance as He sees it.

If I may take a page out of John the Baptist's sermon: Repent! If I may add my own rendition, it would sound something like this: "Repent, and be ye baptized with the Holy Ghost!" And if I were to put it in a plain language version, it would ring this way: "Change the way you think! Ask God to forgive you for a lukewarm spirit! And get filled with the Spirit of God so you can burn and shine again!"

REPENTANCE IS A GIFT

Repentance is a gift. It's not something you earn. It's a gift. When we look at repentance in this light, we'll appreciate it all the more. Repentance is a place where God meets us with His forgiveness and offers us a new beginning. Repentance is where we exchange our wrong mindset for the mind of Christ. Repentance is where we see that we are out of God's perfect will and decide to press in full force to His plan. Repentance is a gift.

Consider the words of Peter as he attempts to explain to the other apostles how the Holy Ghost fell on a household of Gentiles in Joppa:

> Forasmuch then as God gave them the like gift as he did unto us, who believed on the Lord Jesus Christ; what was I, that I could withstand God? When they heard these things, they held their peace, and glorified God, saying, Then hath God also to the Gentiles granted repentance unto life.

> Acts 11:17-19

The Apostle Paul also referenced repentance as a gift from God in his second epistle to Timothy. Let's listen in:

> And the servant of the Lord must not strive; but be gentle unto all men, apt to teach, patient, In meekness instructing those that oppose themselves; if God peradventure will give them repentance to the acknowledging of the truth; And that they may recover themselves out of the snare of the devil, who are taken captive by him at his will.

> 2 Timothy 2:24-26

God is the one who grants repentance unto life. God is the one who grants repentance unto change. So when you think about repentance, think about it as something you receive as much as something you do. True repentance requires faith because without God's grace, without His Spirit, you won't be able to maintain your new way of thinking.

Your willpower alone is not enough to carry you down the narrow path. The opposition is too great. If you want to maintain a fervent spirit, if you want to stay on fire for God, you need to live a lifestyle of repentance. In other words, you need to be sensitive to the Spirit of God so that when you grieve Him, when you miss the mark, when you fall short of the glory of God, you will recognize it quickly. Instead of letting the world, the flesh or the devil put your fire out with the one-two punch of temptation and condemnation, you can repent. When we repent our sins are blotted out and times of refreshing come from the presence of the Lord (Acts 3:19).

ACTIONS SPEAK LOUDER THAN WORDS

Talk is cheap. Actions speak louder than words. You say you've changed. You say you have left the old ways behind. You say you are ready to burn and shine for the Lord. OK, prove it. John the Baptist demanded those who had flowed in a spirit of religion to "bring forth therefore fruits meet for repentance (Matthew 3:8). The Amplified translation puts it this way: "Bring forth fruit that is consistent with repentance [let your lives prove your change of heart].

Yes, the Lord knows your heart. But if what's in your heart is truly different, if you are truly on fire for God, then demonstrating your repentance shouldn't be a worry. If you have really changed, then walking out that change in front of God and man won't be any great challenge. No one expects you to be perfect.

Proving – putting someone to the test – is not a new idea. In the Book of Exodus, we see God proving the Israelites to see if they would diligently hearken to the voice of the Lord and do what was right in His sight, give ear to His commandments and keep all His statues (Exodus 15:24-26). The Israelites didn't do so well on their test. The Bible says the Lord led them 40 years in the wilderness to humble and prove them, to know what was in their heart, whether they would keep His commandments or not (Deuteronomy 8:2).

I submit to you that it didn't have to take 40 years. But their words – their grumbling and complaining – spoke louder than any possible redemptive actions. See, it works both ways. Actions can speak louder than words, but actions come out of the heart. Actions that spring out of the wrong motive are not fruit meet for repentance. Actions that don't spring from a love of God and desire to please Him aren't sustainable.

In other words, you can't keep up the good show forever. And why would you want to? Why would you want to fake it in the Kingdom and let your bones dry out even as you walk down the broad path that leads to destruction when you could sell out and have fire shut up in your bones as you walk the narrow path that leads to life?

The bottom line is this: Out of the abundance of the heart the mouth speaks (Matthew 12:34). If you haven't truly repented your mouth will out you and your pretence won't carry you to the finish line. You can't run the race in a Pharisaical robe. You'll trip over it and fall flat on your face on your way to the Pearly Gates. If you've been acting the part, get a new agent – one that will lead you into repentance, fill you with the Holy Ghost, and put you in your proper role in the Body of Christ. That new agent – the change agent – is Jesus.

GIVING THE LORD LIP SERVICE

God forbid we give the Lord lip service – or not repent quickly. Adam should have repented before the Lord immediately. Instead, he blamed his wife for his sin. Job repented, but he was repenting for the wrong thing at the first. He didn't see his self-righteous spirit, which even manifested in his very repentance. Pharaoh repented and then repented of his repentance. And let's not forget Esau, Jacob's brother.

> Lest there be any fornicator, or profane person, as Esau, who for one morsel of meat sold his birthright. For ye know how that afterward, when he would have inherited the blessing, he was rejected:

for he found no place of repentance,
though he sought it carefully with tears.

Hebrews 12:16-17

Scripture calls him a profane person. Those are pretty serious words against the son of Isaac and grandson of Abraham. But they are indeed fitting. To profane is to treat something sacred with abuse, irreverence or contempt. Why was Esau labeled profane? We know that he shed tears, but they weren't tears of true repentance. Esau cried because he was sorry he missed out on Isaac's blessing for the first-born son. But he wasn't concerned about the blessing when his belly was growling with hunger. He sold it to Jacob and, in doing so, profaned it.

In the end, Esau was not profane because he sinned. He was profane because he didn't truly repent of his sin. He cried over the consequences of the sin rather than his profane acts. Let us not make that same mistake. Let us not only be sorry because we don't like the mess we've gotten ourselves in. Let us be sorry because we grieved the Lord. When we touch His heart with our repentance, we will be forgiven and refreshed. I'm reminded of the words of Paul the apostle after he brought correction to the church at Corinth:

> For though I made you sorry with a
> letter, I do not repent, though I did
> repent: for I perceive that the same

epistle hath made you sorry, though it
were but for a season.

Now I rejoice, not that ye were made
sorry, but that ye sorrowed to
repentance: for ye were made sorry after
a godly manner, that ye might receive
damage by us in nothing. For godly
sorrow worketh repentance to salvation
not to be repented of: but the sorrow of
the world worketh death.

2 Corinthians 7:8-10

I like the New Living translation of verse 10: "For the
kind of sorrow God wants us to experience leads us
away from sin and results in salvation. There's no
regret for that kind of sorrow." Repentance is a good
thing. It cleanses our emotions of the sin-
consciousness and brings prosperity to our souls.
That's important because the Apostle John penned
these words: "Beloved, I wish above all things that
thou mayest prosper and be in health, even as thy soul
prospereth" (3 John 1:2). And with those words in
mind, consider also these words from the Pslamist:

Sing unto the Lord, O ye saints of his,
and give thanks at the remembrance of
his holiness. For his anger endureth but a
moment; in his favour is life: weeping
may endure for a night, but joy cometh

in the morning. And in my prosperity I
said, I shall never be moved.

Psalm 30:4-6

Can you say amen? Repentance is not something to
dread. It's not something to put off. It's not
something to resent. Repentance is what got you
saved in the first place – and it's what's going to keep
you on fire for God. When you stay on fire for God,
you'll see Him respond to that fire. You'll hear His
voice more clearly. You'll have favor with man. You'll
have grace, grace and more grace. You'll maintain
your upper hand over the evil one. A truly repentant
heart get's God's attention every time – and so does a
fervent spirit.

BROKEN, CONTRITE, HUMBLED

As a matter of fact, God is not willing to do without
someone who walks as a broken man or woman
before Him. Your sacrifices and good behavior alone
won't move God. But a humble, broken, contrite
spirit that's overflowing with gratitude and zeal will
touch His heart.

Consider these promises:

> The righteous cry, and the Lord heareth,
> and delivereth them out of all their
> troubles. The Lord is nigh unto them
> that are of a broken heart; and saveth
> such as be of a contrite spirit. Many are

the afflictions of the righteous: but the Lord delivereth him out of them all.

Psalm 34:17-19

And shall say, Cast ye up, cast ye up, prepare the way, take up the stumbling-block out of the way of my people.

For thus saith the high and lofty One that inhabiteth eternity, whose name is Holy; I dwell in the high and holy place, with him also that is of a contrite and humble spirit, to revive the spirit of the humble, and to revive the heart of the contrite ones.

For I will not contend for ever, neither will I be always wroth: for the spirit should fail before me, and the souls which I have made.

Isaiah 57:14-16

Thus saith the Lord, The heaven is my throne, and the earth is my footstool: where is the house that ye build unto me? and where is the place of my rest?

For all those things hath mine hand made, and all those things have been, saith the Lord: but to this man will I

look, even to him that is poor and of a
contrite spirit, and trembleth at my word.

Isaiah 66:1-2

What does it mean to have a broken heart and a
contrite spirit? In this sense, a broken heart is one that
is sorrowful; crushed by the understanding that we
have grieved the Holy Spirit of God. A broken heart
does not make excuses for sin. A broken heart does
not blame people or things its transgressions. A
broken heart is completely subjected to God and His
mercy.

A contrite spirit has a genuine awareness of its
rebellion against God and a determined desire to
change. The good news is where there is a broken
heart and a contrite spirit, God's fire can cleanse,
Jesus' blood can wash white as snow, and the Holy
Spirit can bring about transformation that helps that
one rise up from the ashes of repentance to a new way
of life.

RESISTING THE DEVIL

Staying on fire for God demands self-examination and
repentance, whether you've been saved a week or a
lifetime. For although the enemy's hurricane-force
rains aren't powerful enough to quench the fire of
God in your life, your light spring showers of sin
quench the Spirit every time.

You can't walk in fervent faith and sow to the flesh at the same time. In the Book of Galatians, Paul told us not to grow weary in well doing: for in due season we will reap, if we faint not (Galatians 6:9). He knew the devil would try to weary us, to cause us to get lukewarm and apathetic – and to sin.

Keep in mind that the circumstances the devil throws your way have an end goal in mind: to entice you to sin against God. When you think of it in those terms, I believe it's easier to resist the devil (James 4:7). Why do you think the Scripture says submit yourself to God before it says resist the devil? Because you can't resist the devil if you aren't submitted to God. You need the power of the Holy Ghost to resist the devil and that power demands submission, surrender. If the devil can entice you to sin by your own free will, he doesn't have to flee from you. You've invited him into your circle of friends, so to speak. And he won't flee. He'll keep pulling you further away from God until you are backslidden.

Noteworthy is the verse that precedes Paul's exhortation not to grow weary in well doing: "Be not deceived; God is not mocked: for whatsoever a man soweth, that shall he also reap. For he that soweth to his flesh shall of the flesh reap corruption; but he that soweth to the Spirit shall of the Spirit reap life everlasting" (Galatians 6:10).

Paul told the Romans to stay fervent in spirit, serving the Lord (Romans 12:11). You can't be fervent in spirit if you are continually sowing into the flesh. You can't serve the Lord with your whole heart and simultaneously sow into the flesh. The Bible says the carnal mind is enmity against God (Romans 8:7). Other translations say "the mind of the flesh" or "the wisdom of the flesh."

The flesh has a mind of its own, a wisdom of its own. It's characterized by hostility, rebellion and corruption and it will take you straight to hell if you let it. But thank God, if we do not grow weary in well doing, if we run our race to the end, the corruptible shall put on incorruption, and this mortal shall have put on immortality (1 Corinthians 15:54).

Remember, fervency is a defense against the devil. A fervent lifestyle helps guard your spirit, soul and body from attack in this life, and assures you eternal life when your time on earth is finished.

Before we close this chapter, let us consider David's heartfelt repentance after he committed adultery with Bathsheba and had her husband murdered. I beseech you by the mercies of God not to gloss over this familiar 51st Psalm, but consider the truths therein. I'm not going to expound upon it. David did a better job than I ever could.

> Have mercy upon me, O God, according to thy lovingkindness: according unto the multitude of thy tender mercies blot out

my transgressions. Wash me thoroughly from mine iniquity, and cleanse me from my sin.

For I acknowledge my transgressions: and my sin is ever before me. Against thee, thee only, have I sinned, and done this evil in thy sight: that thou mightest be justified when thou speakest, and be clear when thou judgest. Behold, I was shapen in iniquity; and in sin did my mother conceive me.

Behold, thou desirest truth in the inward parts: and in the hidden part thou shalt make me to know wisdom. Purge me with hyssop, and I shall be clean: wash me, and I shall be whiter than snow.

Make me to hear joy and gladness; that the bones which thou hast broken may rejoice. Hide thy face from my sins, and blot out all mine iniquities. Create in me a clean heart, O God; and renew a right spirit within me. Cast me not away from thy presence; and take not thy holy spirit from me. Restore unto me the joy of thy salvation; and uphold me with thy free spirit.

Then will I teach transgressors thy ways; and sinners shall be converted unto thee. Deliver me from bloodguiltiness, O God, thou God of my salvation: and my tongue shall sing aloud of thy righteousness. O Lord, open thou my lips; and my mouth shall shew forth thy praise.

For thou desirest not sacrifice; else would I give it: thou delightest not in burnt offering. The sacrifices of God are a broken spirit: a broken and a contrite heart, O God, thou wilt not despise. Do good in thy good pleasure unto Zion: build thou the walls of Jerusalem. Then shalt thou be pleased with the sacrifices of righteousness, with burnt offering and whole burnt offering: then shall they offer bullocks upon thine altar.

You can use this prayer as a pattern when you need to repent, so long as you pray it from the heart. You can also encourage yourself with this Psalm after you've repented because it reassures us that God is a God of forgiveness. If that was true in the Old Covenant, how much more so in the New Covenant where the blood of Jesus washes away our sin? Amen.

CHAPTER 7
Remember Where You Came From

Wherefore I say unto thee, Her sins, which are many, are forgiven; for she loved much: but to whom little is forgiven, the same loveth little.

Luke 7:47

Do you remember where you came from? Did you grow up in the church with a silver spoon in your mouth and a sword in your hand that grew rusty because momma did all your fighting for you? Or were you lost in a sewer of sin when God found you, saved you, cleaned you up, blessed you with every spiritual blessing, and gave you a new life you never dreamed was possible? Maybe you are somewhere in the middle of those two extremes.

Here's my point: When you remember where you came from, you'll stir up a love for God that ignites a passion to serve Him. Even if you were born in the church, you know what sin is – and you've committed it. A single sin is enough to separate you from God for all eternity if it had not been for the precious blood of Jesus. Being grateful for our salvation is a sign of humility. Any other attitude is a sign of self-righteousness and a religious spirit.

DO YOU LOVE LITTLE OR MUCH?

The Bible tells the story of a Pharisee (a religious leader in Israel) who asked Jesus to come over for dinner. Jesus accepted the invitation. While He was sitting there, the town harlot came with a bottle of very expensive perfume and stood at His feet, weeping, raining tears on His feet (Luke 7:36-37).

You know the story. She dried His feet, kissed them, and anointed them with perfume. That's when the spirit of religion manifested. The Pharisee said to himself, "If this man was the prophet I thought He was, He would have known what kind of woman this is who is falling all over Him." This self-righteous Pharisee may have said this to himself, but I'm quite sure the look of disgust was all over his face during the woman's act of worship.

Jesus picked up on the thoughts of his heart, and, in His wisdom, turned to Peter with a parable designed to cut to the core of this religious Pharisee. Let's listen in to the wisdom of Jesus.

"Two men were in debt to a banker. One owed five hundred silver pieces, the other fifty. Neither of them could pay up, and so the banker canceled both debts. Which of the two would be more grateful?" Jesus asked.

Simon answered, "I suppose the one who was forgiven the most."

"That's right," said Jesus.

Then turning to the woman, but speaking to Simon, he said, "Do you see this woman? I came to your home; you provided no water for my feet, but she rained tears on my feet and dried them with her hair. You gave me no greeting, but from the time I arrived she hasn't quit kissing my feet. You provided nothing for freshening up, but she has soothed my feet with perfume. Impressive, isn't it? She was forgiven many, many sins, and so she is very, very grateful. If the forgiveness is minimal, the gratitude is minimal."

Luke 7:43-47

The King James translation put it this way: to whom little is forgiven, the same loveth little. Now, the deception is that any of us are better than anyone else. We all have the same sin nature and we've all fallen short of the glory of God. So far as God is concerned, the one who tells an occasional lie and the ax murderer share a common trait: they'll both spend eternity in hell if they don't repent and accept the blood of Christ that takes away our sins.

WHO'S THE CHIEF SINNER?

Listen, it doesn't matter if you grew up in church, started preaching when you were six, married the pastor's daughter and oversee the ushers. We're all utterly lost without the blood of Christ. We have all been forgiven of much – and we should all love much.

Look at the Apostle Paul. He was trained in the Word of God by one of the best Jewish teachers of his day. After his conversion, God used him in a mighty way. His life was transformed from a Christian-persecutor who lived by the letter of the law to Church-builder who lived by the guiding of the Spirit. Yet Paul never forgot where he came from – and his zeal was proof.

> And I thank Christ Jesus our Lord, who hath enabled me, for that he counted me faithful, putting me into the ministry; Who was before a blasphemer, and a persecutor, and injurious: but I obtained mercy, because I did it ignorantly in unbelief.

And the grace of our Lord was exceeding abundant with faith and love which is in Christ Jesus. This is a faithful saying, and worthy of all acceptation, that Christ Jesus came into the world to save sinners; of whom I am chief.

1 Timothy 1:12-15

Paul remembered all to well who he was before he met Christ. I might have to argue with him on one point, though. He thinks he was the chief sinner – I'm sure I was. I thank the Father that He sent His Son to pay the price for my sins. I thank Christ that He was passionate enough about mankind that He was wiling to shed His sinless blood for my sin-stained life. I thank the Holy Spirit that He convicted my heart and showed me that I needed that forgiveness – and sometimes still do.

I OWE YOU MY LIFE

Do you remember the old sitcoms from the 1970s? The "I Owe You My Life" episode was a popular theme back then. I remember one episode of "The Brady Bunch." Peter was just about to get clobbered by a falling ladder when Bobby pushed him out of the way. Peter was so grateful that he volunteered to be Bobby's "slave for life." The same thing happened in "M*A*S*H" when Klinger saved Winchester from an exploding steam generator. In modern times, the theme has even showed up in the popular kids cartoon "Rugrats" when Angelica saves Chuckie's life.

In all those instances, the one being served became a tyrant, taking advantage of the newfound "slave."

Aren't you glad God doesn't do that to us? Before God saved us, we were slaves to sin (Romans 7:14). In this sense of the word, we were completely subservient to the dominating influence of the flesh. The devil was our taskmaster and he was cruel. When we accepted Jesus as our Savior and Lord, we became slaves to God. Paul said it this way:

> Know ye not, that to whom ye yield yourselves servants to obey, his servants ye are to whom ye obey; whether of sin unto death, or of obedience unto righteousness? But God be thanked, that ye were the servants of sin, but ye have obeyed from the heart that form of doctrine which was delivered you. Being then made free from sin, ye became the slaves of righteousness.
>
> Romans 6:16-18

Thanks be to God. I said thanks be to God! Let's continue this passage with the Message translation:

> I'm using this freedom language because it's easy to picture. You can readily recall, can't you, how at servants one time the

more you did just what you felt like doing—not caring about others, not caring about God—the worse your life became and the less freedom you had? And how much different is it now as you live in God's freedom, your lives healed and expansive in holiness?

As long as you did what you felt like doing, ignoring God, you didn't have to bother with right thinking or right living, or right anything for that matter. But do you call that a free life? What did you get out of it? Nothing you're proud of now. Where did it get you? A dead end.

Romans 6:19-20

But now that you've found you don't have to listen to sin tell you what to do, and have discovered the delight of listening to God telling you, what a surprise! A whole, healed, put-together life right now, with more and more of life on the way! Work hard for sin your whole life and your pension is death. But God's gift is real life, eternal life, delivered by Jesus, our Master.

Romans 6:21

ROYAL SERVANTS

God saved our lives. Jesus bought us with a price (1 Corinthians 7:23). But He doesn't lord over us like Pharaoh did to the Israelite he enslaved. No. Far from it. After He redeemed us with His blood and forgave us of our sin, God blessed us with every spiritual blessing in heavenly places in Christ (Ephesians 1:3). He has given us exceeding great and precious promises: that by these we might be partakers of the divine nature, having escaped the corruption that is in the world through lust (2 Peter 1:4). He has given us His authority, His armor, His name and so much more.

Although God is not a harsh taskmaster like Pharaoh, He does have expectations of us. Jesus made it plain when a scribe asked him what is the greatest commandment:

> You shall love the Lord your God with all your heart and with all your soul and with all your mind (intellect). This is the great (most important, principal) and first commandment. And a second is like it: You shall love your neighbor as [you do] yourself. These two commandments sum up and upon them depend all the Law and the Prophets.
>
> Matthew 22:37-40 (AMP)

Think about it for a minute. You were headed for an eternal hellfire. It is a furnace of fire where there will be wailing and gnashing of teeth (Matthew 13:42). It is an everlasting fire prepared for the devil and his angels (Matthew 25:41). It is a fire that shall never be quenched (Mark 9:48). It is a place of tormenting flames (Luke 16:24). It is outer darkness (Matthew 8:12). Hell is an everlasting punishment (Matthew 25:46).

FERVENT BROTHERHOOD

God saved you from this by sending His Son, the Christ, to deliver you from your sinful nature and give you a new nature. If this doesn't cause you to love the Lord your God will all your heart, all your soul, all your mind and all your strength, my friend, you are not only not fervent in spirit, you are ungrateful and probably influenced by a religious spirit of self-righteousness.

Our love for God should be the driving force behind our life. And when it is, we'll manifest a fervent spirit. And when we do, we'll love our neighbors. John, the Apostle of love, put it this way:

> We know that we have passed from death unto life, because we love the brethren. He that loveth not his brother abideth in death. Whosoever hateth his brother is a murderer: and ye know that no murderer hath eternal life abiding in him.

Hereby perceive we the love of God, because he laid down his life for us: and we ought to lay down our lives for the brethren. But whoso hath this world's good, and seeth his brother have need, and shutteth up his bowels of compassion from him, how dwelleth the love of God in him?

My little children, let us not love in word, neither in tongue; but in deed and in truth.

1 John 3:14-18

If you aren't walking in love with your brethren, stop and think about what God has done for you. Think about where you came from and where you would be going if it wasn't for the precious blood of Jesus. Meditate on His saving grace. Your passion will begin to bubble over – and it will be contagious.

NEVER WOULD HAVE MADE IT

There's a song that I love by Marvin Sapp. I love it because it reminds me of God's faithfulness. It puts me in remembrance that God has brought me from a mighty long way. The song is called, "Never Would Have Made It." The lyrics go like this:

Never would have made it, never could have made it, without you
I would have lost it all, but now I see how you were there for me

And I can say
Never would have made it,
Never could have made it,
Without you

I would have lost it all,
But now I see how you were there for
me and I can say
I'm stronger, I'm wiser, I'm better,
Much better,

When I look back over all you
brought me thru.
I can see that you were the one
that
I held on to
And I never
Never would have made it …

It's so easy to get caught up in the daily grind of life. And God has changed us so much, blessed us so much, and promised us so much, that we can easily become fat, comfortable Christians who forgot what it was like to live in our own personal hell on earth. Remembering where you came from will keep your love for God fresh and keep the fire burning.

CHAPTER 8

Practice a Righteousness-Consciousness

For our sake He made Christ [virtually] to be sin Who knew no sin, so that in and through Him we might become [endued with, viewed as being in, and examples of] the righteousness of God [what we ought to be, approved and acceptable and in right relationship with Him, by His goodness].

2 Corinthians 5:21 (AMP)

We may have been chief sinners before we got saved, but now we're the righteousness of God in Christ Jesus. I like how that rolls off my tongue. I like how it rolls off the keyboard, too. Say it out loud with me, "I am the righteousness of God in Christ Jesus." That feels good, doesn't it? Say it once more: "I am the righteousness of God in Christ Jesus."

If you want to say on fire for God, you need to learn how to practice a righteousness-conscious instead of a sin-consciousness. A person with a sin-consciousness focuses more the sin he commits than the righteousness he has in Christ. Don't get me wrong, when we sin we need to have a contrite spirit. We need to repent. But we don't need to stay focused on that sin after we've truly repented. We need to move on by faith that God has forgiven us whether we feel forgiven or not. To continue to beat yourself up over a sin that God has already forgiven you of is to commit yet another sin: the sin of unbelief.

By inspiration of the Holy Spirit, the Apostle John wrote, "If we confess our sins, He is faithful and just to forgive us our sins, and to cleanse us from all unrighteousness" (1 John 1:9). The Preacher wrote, "He who conceals his transgressions will not prosper, but he who confesses and forsakes them will find compassion" (Proverbs 28:13). The Psalmist wrote, "As far as the east is from the west, so far has he removed our transgressions from us" (Psalm 103:12). Again, when you confess your sin, you need to receive forgiveness by faith. If you keep beating yourself up over the same old sin, you are walking in unbelief and, my friends, that's a sin.

YOU ARE ACCEPTED IN THE BELOVED

Can you see how the devil twists this up? If the enemy can get you so focused on what a wretched sinner you are, then you won't rise up in the righteousness of God and fulfill your destiny. You'll be too focused on yourself and your sin to focus on really helping anybody else. Your motivations will be to make up for what you did wrong rather than serving God out of a pure heart of love alone.

I used to beat myself bloody over every little mistake I made. I would spend my time with God rehearsing my mistakes and asking Him, "What's the matter with me?" I would sit at His feet and berate, bludgeon and belittle myself time and time again. Needless to say, I didn't feel to good about myself. I felt like a failure. The devil had me right where he wanted me.

I guess the Lord eventually got tired of the routine. One day He said this to me, "Would you just stop it?" That startled me because in my mind I was merely repenting for sin. But it wasn't repentance I was engaging in. It was an ongoing rehearsal of all my shortcomings. I was practicing my sin-consciousness in front of an audience of three: Father, Son and Holy Ghost. None of them appreciated the repeat performances.

So the Lord had my attention, and He asked me a second question: "How would you like to sit and watch your daughter beat herself up every day?" I didn't have to think about that one very long. Of course, no loving mother would sit by and watch her child beat herself up day in and day out. Well, no loving Father would either. God had been trying to get through to me for I don't know how long before the light broke through. Sometimes it's hard to hear the Spirit of the Lord when you are wallowing in self-pity.

I replied, "I wouldn't."

His answer? "I don't like it either. Stop beating yourself up all the time. Go read Ephesians 1:6."

Well, I have to admit, I didn't remember off hand what Ephesians 1:6 said. But I'll never forget it again. So I got off my knees and grabbed my Bible. I turned to the first Chapter of the Book of Ephesians and looked for the sixth verse. Do you know what it says: "To the praise of the glory of his grace, wherein he hath made us accepted in the beloved."

As soon as I had finished reading the words on the page, the Spirit said, "I accept you just the way you are." The Lord doesn't expect us to be perfect. He already knew every sin you'd commit before He saved you. He already knows every word that will come out of your mouth before you speak it. Nothing we do is any surprise to God. That doesn't give us a license to sin, rather it sets us free from the guilt of sinning because we can simply repent and move on.

WHO YOU ARE IN CHRIST

If you want to maintain a righteousness-conscious, you need to get a revelation of you are in Christ. If you take the time to study this out, or if you go on the

Internet and type in "Who I am in Christ," you'll find a list of Scriptures that will help you settle the matter in your heart. Meditate on Scriptures about who you are in Christ every day until it comes up out of your spirit when the world and the devil try to beat you down.

When you do this, what you'll find is that you are accepted, secure and significant. You are complete in Christ (Colossians 2:9-10). You have been redeemed and forgiven of all your sins (Colossians 1:13-14). You have been justified (Romans 5:1). You are united with the Lord and one with Him in Spirit (1 Corinthians 6:17).

You are also free from condemnation (Romans 8:1-2). You cannot be separated from the love of God (Romans 8:31-39). You can be confident that God will complete the good work He started in you (Philippians 1:6). And since you are born of God the evil one cannot touch you (1 John 5:18).

You are God's workmanship (Ephesians 2:10). You are God's temple (1 Corinthians 3:16). You are a branch of Jesus Christ, the true vine, and a channel of His life (John 15:5). You are seated with Him in heavenly places (Ephesians 2:6).

Doesn't it make you feel good to know that? "Religious" people don't want you to know that. They want you walk around trying to pay for your sin.

But I'm here to tell you that you are the righteousness of God in Christ Jesus. When you realize who you are in Christ and what belongs to the righteous, you'll fan the flames of the fire within you. Indeed, you'll maintain a fervent spirit and that fire will spread. The key is really knowing who you are in Him and the blessings of the righteous.

SOLOMON'S TAKE ON RIGHTEOUSNESS

The Book of Proverbs has plenty to say about the righteous and the wicked. So as we practice becoming righteousness-conscious instead of sin-conscious, Proverbs is a great faith-builder. You'll begin to expect the benefits of righteousness as Solomon laid them out, and you'll begin to walk in them. As you do, your will become even more fervent in spirit.

Consider some of the benefits for the righteous. And as you meditate these Scriptures, remember that you are the righteousness of God in Christ. Every one of these statements is true for you:

A Strong Connection with God

God lays up sound wisdom for the **righteous** (Proverbs 2:7).

God's secret is with the **righteous** (Proverbs 3:32).

The lips of the **righteous** know what is acceptable (Proverbs 10:32).

God hears the prayer of the **righteous**
(Proverbs 15:29).

Protection & Deliverance

Righteousness delivers from death
(Proverbs 10:2).

The Lord will not suffer the soul of the
righteous to famish (Proverbs 10:3).

The wages of **righteousness** is life
(Proverbs 10:6).

The **righteous** shall never be removed
(Proverbs 10:30).

The **righteousness** of the blameless
makes a straight way for them (Proverbs
11:15).

The **righteous** is delivered out of trouble
(Proverbs 11:8).

The wicked bow at the gates of the
righteous (Proverbs 14:19).

The name of the Lord is a strong tower:
the **righteous** run into it and are safe
(Proverbs 18:10).

The **righteous** are as bold as a lion
(Proverbs 28:1).

Blessings Galore

The desire of the **righteous** shall be
granted (Proverbs 10:24).

The hope of the **righteous** shall be gladness (Proverbs 10:28).

The **righteous** shall flourish as a branch (Proverbs 11:28).

The **righteous** shall be recompensed in the earth (Proverbs 11:31).

The house of the **righteous** shall stand (Proverbs 12:7).

Among the **righteous** there is favor (Proverbs 14:9).

He that follows after **righteousness** and mercy finds life, **righteousness**, and honor (Proverbs 21:21).

Blessing Others

The mouth of a **righteous** man is well of life (Proverbs 10:11).

The lips of the **righteous** feed many (Proverbs 10:21).

The **righteous** is an everlasting foundation (Proverbs 10:25).

In the house of the **righteous** is much treasure (Proverbs 15:6).

Can you see it? If focusing on your righteousness in Christ and the benefits of the righteous doesn't cause you to praise God with all that's in you, then you aren't getting it – or you are merely taking it for granted. That's a major issue in the Body of Christ.

We can't have faith for something we take for granted.

We sometimes get so familiar with the Word of God that we allow the devil to breed contempt in our hearts. We become so familiar with a verse – or God forbid even God Himself – that we no longer reverence the Word or the Spirit among us. That causes us to become careless – and that is dangerous.

The Preacher wrote, "For the backsliding of the simply shall slay them, and the careless ease of [self-confident] fools shall destroy them" (Proverbs 1:32 AMP). Let us not get familiar or careless with the things of God. Let us rather demonstrate a fear of the Lord. Let us work out our salvation with fear and trembling (Philippians 2:12). Familiarity quenches the fire, but the fear of the Lord ignites it.

CHAPTER 9
Forget Not All His Benefits

O my soul, bless God From head to toe, I'll bless his holy name! O my soul, bless God, don't forget a single blessing!

Psalm 103:1-2 (MSG)

Just as remembering where you came from stirs up your zeal, remembering all of your newfound benefits fans the flames of your fervency.

Think about it for a minute. If all God ever did was save us from an eternity separated from Him, that would be more than enough. But God in His mercy with the great love with which He loves us, didn't stop there. As citizens of the Kingdom, we have a benefits package that beats what any Fortune 500 company has ever or could ever offer.

Indeed, the Bible offers some 7,000 promises that cover our life from cradle to grave – and beyond the grave into eternity with Him. Sometimes in the daily grind of life, when circumstances that defy God's promises attempt to chase us down and overtake us, it's easy to forget our benefits. That's why we need to review some of them every day. We need to be able to tell the devil what's in our benefits package when he comes with his stealing, killing and destroying agenda.

FERVENT MEDITATION

We often meditate on God's instructions – God's commandments to us – and we should absolutely do that. In order to be successful Kingdom citizens, we need to understand the principles and boundaries of our domain. But I think sometimes we neglect to meditate on His benefits, His promises, His absolute guarantees for those who believe. A good place to start is Psalm 103:

> Bless the Lord, O my soul: and all that is within me, bless his holy name. Bless the Lord, O my soul, and forget not all his benefits:

> Who forgiveth all thine iniquities; who healeth all thy diseases; Who redeemeth thy life from destruction; who crowneth thee with lovingkindness and tender mercies; Who satisfieth thy mouth with good things; so that thy youth is renewed like the eagle's.

The Lord executeth righteousness and judgment for all that are oppressed. He made known his ways unto Moses, his acts unto the children of Israel. The Lord is merciful and gracious, slow to anger, and plenteous in mercy.

He will not always chide: neither will he keep his anger forever. He hath not dealt with us after our sins; nor rewarded us according to our iniquities. For as the heaven is high above the earth, so great is his mercy toward them that fear him. As far as the east is from the west, so far hath he removed our transgressions from us. Like as a father pitieth his children, so the Lord pitieth them that fear him. For he knoweth our frame; he remembereth that we are dust.

As for man, his days are as grass: as a flower of the field, so he flourisheth. For the wind passeth over it, and it is gone; and the place thereof shall know it no more. But the mercy of the Lord is from everlasting to everlasting upon them that fear him, and his righteousness unto children's children; To such as keep his covenant, and to those that remember his commandments to do them. The Lord hath prepared his throne in the heavens; and his kingdom ruleth over all.

Bless the Lord hath prepared his throne in the heavens; and his kingdom ruleth over all. Bless the Lord, ye his angels, that excel in strength, that do his commandments, hearkening unto the voice of his word. Bless ye the Lord hath prepared his throne in the heavens; and his kingdom ruleth over all.

Bless the Lord, all ye his hosts; ye ministers of his, that do his pleasure. Bless the Lord hath prepared his throne in the heavens; and his kingdom ruleth over all. Bless the Lord, all his works in all places of his dominion: bless the Lord hath prepared his throne in the heavens; and his kingdom ruleth over all. Bless the Lord, O my soul.

Can you se the natural response to "forgetting not all of His benefits?" Blessing the Lord. When we meditate on God's promises, it should light a fire in our hearts for Him. We should bless His holy name. We should exalt Him and praise Him and worship Him and glorify Him. It should cause us to want to serve Him all the more. And these are just a few of the promises of God. Whatever need you have, spirit, soul or body, God has a promise that covers it. All you have to do is believe with a fervent faith.

STARTING IN THE FLESH

When I say meditate, I don't just mean to read it out of your Bible. I mean to say it out of your mouth. Do both. If you put the Word of God in your eyes, your ears and your mouth, you will see results. That's a guarantee.

More days than one, confessing the Word kept me from giving up, throwing in the towel, calling it quits, walking away. Sometimes the battle gets intense. But that's exactly why we need a fervent spirit. When the battle heats up, our spirits should rise to the occasion and display our fervency in Christ all the more. But you need the Word of God to feed your fervency. Let me say that again: You need the Word of God to feed your fervency. The Word is sort of like kindling for a fire, in some respects. If your fire is starting to go out, throw some Word on it and see what happens.

I can be having the worst day in the world, but when I begin confessing the Word of God the spiritual climate around me begins to change. I have a confession list that's pages and pages long. Sure, I sometimes start out reading it in monotone, without any fervor whatsoever. I'm just reading words on a page by faith in the midst of a mind battle.

But after I make my way down through a few of those promises, I can feel my spirit rising within me. My monotone changes to full stereo and the fervency begins to bubble. By the time I've made my way down to the bottom of the first page, I'm declaring the Word of God over my life with great confidence and boldness. Before you know it, the devil has fled. He grew weary of hearing me. My fervent spirit resisted his attacks and he had no choice but to flee.

So next time you are having a bad day, grab your Bible and start reading it out loud. If you don't have a confession list, make one. You may start off reading it in the flesh, but I guarantee you'll end up in the heights of the spirit because faith comes by hearing the Word of God.

CHAPTER 10
Developing a Lifestyle of Prayer

Pray at all times (on every occasion, in every season) in the
Spirit, with all [manner of] prayer and entreaty. To that end
keep alert and watch with strong purpose and perseverance,
interceding in behalf of all the saints (God's consecrated people).

Ephesians 6:18

There are two sides of the prayer equation. If you are
on fire for God, your prayer life will be fervent. And if
you aren't on fire for God, fervent prayer will ignite
the flames of passion in your spirit. Remember, prayer
is simply taking to God – and listening as He talks to
you. Prayer is asking for God's will in the earth and
believing He will answer.

Prayer is your connection with God. Answered prayer
brings glory to the Father (John 14:13-14). Answered
prayer brings fruit (John 15:7-8). Answered prayer
gives us joy (John 16:23-24). I submit to you that if

you are seeing God answer your prayers, you are seeing glorious fruit for the Kingdom that brings your heart great joy and stirs within you a passion for prayer.

It's not hard to develop a lifestyle of prayer when you are seeing prayer answers left and right. It's when we aren't seeing the apparent prayer answers that the devil tempts us with weariness. But fervent faith in God fans the flames and stirs up the gift, praying with understanding and praying in the Spirit because fervent faith isn't selfish. Fervent faith knows that if it labors in prayer to bring God's will to pass in the earth, all of our needs will be taken care of in more-than-enough style.

THE PRAYER LINES ARE OPEN

There is no lack of prayer lines you can call – or even e-mail – these days. And thank God for them. We can all use someone to touch and agree with us from time to time and, let's face it, our pastor and our best friend aren't always available in the midnight hour. But the best news of all is that with God, the prayer lines are always open. A fervent spirit maintains the connection morning, noon and night.

See, it's not necessarily about praying for an hour. I'm not discouraging prayer meetings in any sense of the word. My point is, if we have a fervent spirit we'll be talking to God throughout the day, lifting up petitions for help along the way. We won't reserve prayer for the prayer meeting only. We won't relegate prayer to

the prayer hour, but we'll burst through those
boundaries and pray fervently, even when fervently is
quietly, as the Spirit leads.

That's what Paul the apostle meant when he said,
"Pray without ceasing" (1 Thessalonians 5:17). Prayer
becomes as natural as breathing. It's not just
something we set aside a special time for. It's also
something we do as part of our spirit-nature. And
indeed you have to depend on your spirit nature to
remain on fire for God, fervent in prayer. Jesus said,
"Watch and pray, that ye enter not into temptation:
the spirit indeed is willing, but the flesh is weak"
(Matthew 26:41).

Paul also said to continue instant in prayer (Romans
12:12). And to pray always with all prayer and
supplication in the Spirit, and watching thereunto with
all perseverance and supplication for all saints"
(Ephesians 6:18). When you are constantly praying,
you are constantly talking to God. You are
strengthening your relationship with him. You are
keeping the fire burning.

PRAYING IN THE SPIRIT

Paul also said we know not what we should pray for
as we ought (Romans 8:26). That's OK because the
Holy Ghost knows how to pray. Aren't you glad the
Spirit helps our weaknesses? Aren't you glad you have
a supernatural connection with God that allows you to
pray a perfect prayer even when you don't know how
to pray? Aren't you glad you can pray in the Spirit and

pray with the understanding also? (1 Corinthians 14:15). When you pray in the spirit you fan the flames of your fervency. I don't know how it works, but it does.

You can also build yourself up in your most holy, most fervent faith by praying in tongues. Allowing the Holy Ghost to pray through you will edify your spirit and ensure perfect prayers are being released on your behalf (Jude 1:20). When doubt hits my mind, or when I don't know what to do, I pray in tongues. When my spirit is edified, it's so much easier to catch those doubtful imaginations before they have time to take root.

Remember, the parable of the Sower? (Mark 4:1-20). The Sower who sowed the Word was Jesus, but I believe the devil is also sowing words; words of doubt and unbelief and fear and insecurity. Praying in tongues will help us to keep our spirits receptive to the things of God, and, in doing so, guard our hearts and minds in Christ Jesus. Think of praying in tongues as making your shield of faith even stronger, wider, taller than it already is. If you aren't baptized in the Holy Spirit, pray and ask God to fill you to overflowing. Jesus is the Baptizer and He will respond to your hunger and thirst to be filled with the Holy Spirit who will lead and guide you into truth instead of doubt.

What's more, the Apostle Paul offered some awesome insight to the church at Corinth: "For he that speaketh in an unknown tongue speaketh not unto men, but unto God: for no man understandeth him; howbeit in the spirit he speaketh mysteries" (1 Corinthians 14:2). Praying in tongues make will help shape your destiny. Praying in tongues opens up your spirit to more revelation from the Lord so that we can walk on His path with a knowing the devil can't take away.

DEVELOPING A LIFESTYLE OF PRAYER

You probably agree with all that's been said, but the question lingers in your mind: "How can I develop a lifestyle of prayer? I get up before the crack of dawn to get the kids ready for school. I rush to work and am stuck in meetings all day. I get home just in time to cook dinner for my family and pick up around the house. And I fall asleep exhausted so I can repeat the routine tomorrow. I have a lifestyle of meeting the needs of my family. How does that fit in with a lifestyle of prayer?" The answer is, quite nicely.

If you lead a harried, hectic life, you have a head start in your quest to develop a lifestyle of prayer because the first requirement is humility. When we realize that apart from Christ we can do nothing, we will ask the Father for help with everything. We won't attempt to rush out on our own without petitioning the Lord for His grace, His direction, His strength. To be sure, the humble heart is the prayerful heart and the prayerful heart is one that is on fire for the God whose ability makes up for our inability. Consider the contrast between the religious spirit and the fervent spirit.

Two men went up into the temple [enclosure] to pray, the one a Pharisee and the other a tax collector. The Pharisee took his stand ostentatiously and began to pray thus before and with himself: God, I thank You that I am not like the rest of men—extortioners (robbers), swindlers [unrighteous in heart and life], adulterers--or even like this tax collector here. I fast twice a week; I give tithes of all that I gain.

But the tax collector, [merely] standing at a distance, would not even lift up his eyes to heaven, but kept striking his breast, saying, O God, be favorable (be gracious, be merciful) to me, the especially wicked sinner that I am!

I tell you, this man went down to his home justified (forgiven and made upright and in right standing with God), rather than the other man; for everyone who exalts himself will be humbled, but he who humbles himself will be exalted.

Luke 18:9-14 (AMP)

There are many different types of prayer. We won't get into them all here. Suffice it to say that developing a lifestyle of prayer means different things at different times. Sometimes you are praying a prayer of consecration to consecrate yourself to God's will in a matter. Other times you are praying a prayer of repentance. Still other times you are praying the prayer of faith for the sick. If you are going to develop a lifestyle of prayer, it doesn't hurt to understand that there are many different types of prayer for many different occasions.

You wouldn't do spiritual warfare over Thanksgiving dinner, would you? But you wouldn't pray a prayer of consecration over your financial wellbeing when you know clearly know that God's will is for you to prosper. Using the right prayer at the right time will produce the best results. When you begin to see prayer answers, you will be encouraged to continue in the lifestyle of prayer you are pursuing.

AMPING UP YOUR PRAYER LIFE

Of course, there are volumes that could be written on this topic. For our purposes, we'll just review some of the ingredients for developing a lifestyle of prayer – effective, fervent prayer that availeth much.

For starters, spending time in the Word of God is a must. We need to pray according to the will of God, which is expressed in His Word. If we aren't putting the Word in us, the Word won't come out of us. We can't rely on yesterday's manna. We need a fresh experience with the Word of God every day. Reading the Word of God should stir you to pray, and praying should stir a hunger to consume the Word of God.

Next, spend time with the Spirit of God. The Holy Spirit is here on the earth. Jesus sent Him as our Comforter, Counselor, Helper, Intercessor, Advocate, Strengthener and Standby – and He remains with us forever (John 14:15-16). You should fellowship with the Holy Spirit. He is just as much God as the Father and Jesus are God, but He is too often ignored. It's the Holy Spirit that stirs the fire of God in your belly. Talk to Him, adore Him, worship Him. Ask Him to help you develop a lifestyle of prayer. A stronger prayer life will be the result.

Praying is an act of your will. No one can make you pray. You have to be determined to cultivate a lifestyle of prayer because the enemy certainly doesn't want to see you walking in the spirit of prayer. When we pray, we do damage to his kingdom, we edify ourselves, we change the course of lives – we make an impact.

Consider the words of Smith Wigglesworth, that great British healing evangelist: Smith Wigglesworth once said, "I never pray for more than 30 minutes, but I never go more than 30 minutes without praying." See, it's not necessarily about praying for hours on end. It's about continuing in prayer. As you do, you'll maintain a fervent spirit because you are continually connected to the Living God.

CHAPTER 11
Practice the Presence of God

Let us come before his presence with thanksgiving, and make a joyful noise unto him with psalms.

Psalm 95:2

If practice makes perfect, does practicing the presence of God perfect you? I think it does. I believe the more time we spend in God's glory, the more we change from glory to glory, the more His fire purges the impurities in our lives, and more fervent we become for our Lord.

So the question is, how do we practice the presence of God. Have you ever read "The Practice of the Presence of God"? The book documents the conversations and letters of a monk named Brother Lawrence who proved that there truly is fullness of joy in His presence (Psalm 16:11). Brother Lawrence, born as Nicholas Herman of Lorraine, was a lowly and unlearned man. He died in 1691 at the age of 80. But he left us with wisdom for the ages.

Brother Lawrence was on fire for God. He said, this: "I did not engage in a religious life but for the love of God, and I have endeavored to act only for Him; whatever becomes of me, whether I be lost or saved, I will always continue to act purely for the love of God. I shall have this good at least, that til death I shall have done all that is in me to love him."

ENTERING HIS PRESENCE

God is everywhere. Everywhere. Everywhere. David asked, "Whither shall I go from thy spirit? or whither shall I flee from thy presence? (Psalm 139:7) It was a rhetorical question. The answer is nowhere, because God is everywhere. In fact, He dwells within our spirits. So why is it so difficult at times to enter into His presence? One answer, in a nutshell, is distractions.

I understand all too well that it's all too easy to get distracted by the daily demands of life. And when those demands subside it's tempting to continue thinking about the demands of tomorrow. That's why Jesus said, "Do not worry about tomorrow; for tomorrow will care for itself. Each day has enough trouble of its own" (Matthew 6:34 NASB).

In order to enter the presence of God – or rather realize the presence of God in your life – you have to cast all your cares on the Lord. You need to let go of the daily woes you've faced. You need to take your weary, burdened soul to Jesus so He can give you rest (Matthew 11:28-30). You need to forget about yourself and your problems and focus on Jesus and His majesty. Sometimes you have to struggle with both flesh and soul to get there, but if you just begin thanking Him you'll soon break through. You may need to repent. If so do it, receive your forgiveness, and get to thanking.

> Psalm 100:4 says, "Enter into his gates with thanksgiving, and into his courts with praise: be thankful unto him, and bless his name."

> Psalm 95:2 says, "Let us come before his presence with thanksgiving, and make a joyful noise unto him with psalms."

> Psalm 100:2 says, "Serve the Lord with gladness: come before his presence with singing."

> Psalm 96:2 says, "Sing to the Lord, bless His name; Proclaim good tidings of His salvation from day to day."

> Psalm 116:17 says, "To You I shall
> offer a sacrifice of thanksgiving, And
> call upon the name of the Lord."

Praise and worship should not be relegated to Sunday morning. If you want to practice the presence of God, you'll need to maintain an attitude of thanksgiving, praise and worship 24/7/365. The Bible says, in view of God's mercy, that we should present our bodies as living sacrifices, holy and pleasing to God – this is our spiritual act of worship (Romans 12:1).

So what are you waiting for? We'll talk more about giving thanks in the next chapter, but this should get give you something to meditate on in the meantime. Go ahead and start thanking Him now. Start praising Him now. Start worshiping Him now. You'll be glad you did!

RESPONDING TO HIS PRESENCE

Not everybody responds the same to the presence of God. Adam and Eve hid themselves from the presence of the Lord God in the trees of the Garden of Eden after they sinned (Genesis 3:8).

Isn't that what we do sometimes? When we miss the mark, we sometimes feel so bad about ourselves that we don't want to get into the presence of God. We don't feel worthy. We feel ashamed. That's the wrong response. When we fall short of the glory of God, and we all do, we need to repent and get back into the glory of God so we can receive forgiveness, refreshing and strengthening lest practice the sin we committed instead of practicing the presence of the Forgiver we serve.

We should respond to the presence of God with reverence and a worshipful fear of the Lord. The earth trembles at the presence of the Lord – how much more should we? (Psalm 114:7)

> Fear ye not me? saith the Lord: will ye not tremble at my presence, which have placed the sand for the bound of the sea by a perpetual decree, that it cannot pass it: and though the waves thereof toss themselves, yet can they not prevail; though they roar, yet can they not pass over it?
>
> Jeremiah 5:22

Let us not be irreverent in the presence of the Lord. The Lord is due respect, honor, glory, praise, worship, thanksgiving and much more than we can ever offer. When we reverence the Lord as we stand in His presence, we enjoy so many benefits that we can't access any other way.

> How great is your goodness, which you have stored up for those who fear you, which you bestow in the sight of men on those who take refuge in you.

In the shelter of your presence you
hide them from the intrigues of men;
in your dwelling you keep them safe
from accusing tongues.

Psalm 31:19-20

Also consider Psalm 91. It's a promise to those who
dwell in the secret place of the Most High. Confess it
out of your mouth every day. It will lead you into
thanksgiving, praise, worship – and into a realization
of His presence.

The Bible also says glory and honor are in His
presence; strength and gladness are in His place (1
Chronicles 16:27). When we come boldly to the
throne of grace, we find there, in His presence, grace
and mercy to help in a time of need (Hebrews 4:16).
There is help in the battle in the presence of the Lord
(Psalm 9:3; Psalm 31:20). Times of refreshing come
from the presence of the Lord (Acts 3:19).

WAITING UPON THE LORD

Moses wasn't willing to move on without the presence
of God in his life. He knew the task was too great to
forge ahead without the Spirit of Grace (Exodus
33:13-15). Moses did something we should do: He
asked for God's to show him His ways. David had a
similar prayer request. This should be atop our prayer
list, too: "Shew me thy ways, O Lord; teach me thy
paths. Lead me in thy truth, and teach me: for thou art

the God of my salvation; on thee do I wait all the day (Psalm 25:4-5).

Waiting upon the Lord. The Prophet Isaiah offers words of encouragement to the weary; those who need a refreshing from the presence of God. If that's you, if you are experiencing burn out, let this Scripture burn in your heart unto revival.

> Have you not known? Have you not heard? The everlasting God, the Lord, the Creator of the ends of the earth, does not faint or grow weary; there is no searching of His understanding.
>
> He gives power to the faint and weary, and to him who has no might He increases strength [causing it to multiply and making it to abound].
>
> Even youths shall faint and be weary, and [selected] young men shall feebly stumble and fall exhausted; But those who wait for the Lord [who expect, look for, and hope in Him] shall change and renew their strength and power; they shall lift their wings and mount up [close to God] as eagles [mount up to the sun]; they shall run and not be weary, they shall walk and not faint or become tired.
>
> Isaiah 40:28-31 (AMP)

What does it mean to wait upon the Lord? I like the Amplified Bible translation of this verse because it expounds on the topic to bring more understanding. Waiting on the Lord isn't merely sitting in your prayer closet staring at a wall. The Lord responds to our faith. Faith flows in expectation. If you invited a friend to dinner at 7 p.m., you would have faith that he would show up. You would expect him there on time. And you would begin looking for him in anticipation a few minutes before 7 p.m.

That's what we must do as we wait upon the Lord. We must expect Him to show up. We must look for Him; discern His presence round and about us for He is really and truly always with us. We just don't recognize His presence. As be begin to practice His presence, we'll spend less time "waiting" and more time fellowshipping with the Spirit of God.

You have plenty of incentive to wait upon the Lord and to practice His presence. There are promises to those who wait upon the Lord. The first promise is we will change. I believe as we stand – or kneel or lay prostrate – in His presence, we open the door to allow the Holy Spirit to change us, to turn our hearts, to lead us into the next place He has for us.

Next, the Bible says we will renew our strength and power. Our strength and power come from the Lord. Our own physical might and our own physical power won't get us very far when the devil is attacking. We need the strength and power that comes from the Spirit of God.

The Bible also says those who wait upon the Lord will mount up with wings as eagles – close to God. In this I see prophetic perspective. In other words, when we wait upon the Lord, we'll begin to get His perspective on things. And believe me, His perspective is much better than ours. When we're in the midst of a battle – when the enemy is up in our face – it can be difficult to see the big picture. But when we wait upon the Lord we mount up with wings as eagles, far above the circumstances that are trying to quench the fire of God in our lives, and we see things as God sees them. When we do, it sparks new fire in our hearts.

Finally, the Bible says if we wait upon the Lord, we shall run and not grow weary, walk and not faint or become tired. What a promise! If this is true of waiting upon the Lord, it is also true of practicing the presence of God. When we practice His presence, the devil won't bowl us over with the spirit of weariness in effort to get us to faint in the midst of our well doing so we don't reap the reward of obedience. Praise the Lord!

When we practice the presence of God, we can live in these promises because we are constantly waiting upon Him. We are constantly expecting Him to speak or lead us by His Spirit. We are constantly looking for Him in all that we do.

QUENCHING HIS PRESENCE

The Bible speaks clearly about not suppressing the Spirit. Some translations of 1 Thessalonians 5:19 say don't quench the Spirit. Others say don't subdue the Spirit. Still others say don't stifle the Spirit. The translation I like the best is, "Do not put out the Spirit's fire."

Can you imagine? The Spirit brings fire with Him. We put out that fire by practicing sin rather than practicing His presence. We put out that fire by failing to fear the Lord. We put out that fire by taking His presence for granted. If we put out the Spirit's fire, we're putting out our own fire, too, and if we don't throw some fuel on our fire in a hurry we'll wax lukewarm and eventually grow cold. God forbid.

David watched Saul put out the Spirit's fire and he knew his sin with Bathsheba had thrown cold water all over his own ministry. He didn't want to lose the Spirit of God like Saul did. In his repentance for committing adultery and murder, David cried out to God, "Cast me not away from thy presence; and take not thy Holy Spirit from me" (Psalm 51:11). David knew that apart from Him, he could do nothing and he was desperate to return to the fellowship he once had with the Spirit of God.

Then there's Jonah. This stubborn prophet was so willful and disobedient that he actually ran from God's presence rather than completing his God-given mission.

> But Jonah rose up to flee unto Tarshish from the presence of the Lord, and went down to Joppa; and he found a ship going to Tarshish: so he paid the fare thereof, and went down into it, to go with them unto Tarshish from the presence of the Lord.

Jonah 1:3

Well, we all know Jonah's fate. He ended up in the belly of the whale and there repented. But then he repented of his repentance and sat under a tree wishing he would die. There is no record in the Bible of God ever using Jonah again after the pride in his heart served as a snare to his soul.

HUMILITY OR HUBRIS?

The devil used to be the worship leader. He used to be in God's presence all the time. But his pride ejected Him from the presence of God. Our pride will do the same.

When we walk in a prideful attitude, the Spirit of God is repelled. It's the same sin Lucifer committed and God hasn't changed His mind about its filth. The good news is as we practice the presence of God we'll become humbler. As we maintain a greater awareness that He is everywhere and He is with us, to lead us and guide us and help us and change us, we won't be so apt to sit in judgment of our brothers and sisters, let corrupt speech come out of our mouths, play childish relationship games, or commit other sins we may take for granted.

CHAPTER 12
Giving Thanks Always

In every thing give thanks: for this is the will of God in Christ Jesus concerning you.

1 Thessalonians 5:18

Jesus gave Himself for us that He might redeem us from every lawless deed and purify for Himself His own special people, zealous for good works (Titus 2:14). God expects us to be zealous for good works. He expects us to be thankful that He redeemed us and purified us.

Unfortunately, too many of us act like spoiled brats. Rather than being thankful that we aren't going to spend an eternity in hell, we get annoyed because we've been waiting six months for an answer to prayer. I submit to you that if we were more thankful for what we do have, we could access more of what we want to have. If we were more grateful for our family, we would have better family relationships. If we were more grateful for our jobs, we might get that promotion we've been seeking. If we were more grateful for our salvation, we might walk in greater spiritual authority. Skeptical? Why not try it? What do you have to lose?

In fact, you should do more than try it. You should live it. In his first epistle to the church at Thessalonica, the Apostle Paul exhorted the people to give thanks in every thing, noting that such is the will of God in Christ Jesus (1 Thessalonians 5:18). The Apostle Paul repeated his exhortation in the book of Ephesians when he wrote, "Giving thanks always for all things unto God and the Father in the name of our Lord Jesus Christ" (Ephesians 5:20).

THANKING GOD THROUGH THE STORM

Before you take exception, Paul wasn't saying to give thanks for everything in the sense that God brought it upon you. Every good and perfect gift comes from Him. If a loved ones dies or you get into a bad car accident, you don't need to thank the Lord for that because He's not the one who steals, kills and destroys. It wasn't God that killed your loved one or caused you to wreck your car. But you can still thank God "in" every thing.

You can still thank God that He's going to bring something good out of it. The Bible says that God works all things together for good to them that love God, to them who are the called according to His purpose (Romans 8:28). As you are going through good times and bad, thank Him. A thankful spirit is a fervent spirit.

> As ye have therefore received Christ Jesus the Lord, so walk ye in him: Rooted and built up in him, and stablished in the faith, as ye have been taught, abounding therein with thanksgiving.
>
> Colossians 2:6-7

Paul told us this for our own good. God doesn't need our thanks. He's God whether we thank Him or not. An attitude of gratitude will keep you humble. And God gives grace to the humble. The Holy Spirit told me once that an attitude problem is a gratitude problem. When we don't walk in humility, we've got the wrong attitude. Do you remember the lepers that Jesus healed? Most of them were ungrateful. I sometimes wonder how many of them kept their healing.

> And it came to pass, as he went to Jerusalem, that he passed through the midst of Samaria and Galilee.
>
> And as he entered into a certain village, there met him ten men that were lepers, which stood afar off: And they lifted up

their voices, and said, Jesus, Master, have mercy on us.

And when he saw them, he said unto them, Go shew yourselves unto the priests. And it came to pass, that, as they went, they were cleansed.

And one of them, when he saw that he was healed, turned back, and with a loud voice glorified God, And fell down on his face at his feet, giving him thanks: and he was a Samaritan.

And Jesus answering said, Were there not ten cleansed? but where are the nine? There are not found that returned to give glory to God, save this stranger. And he said unto him, Arise, go thy way: thy faith hath made thee whole.

Luke 17:11-19

THE SIN OF INGRATITUDE

Fervent faith is thankful. It's thankful all the time, not just when it needs something. Fervent faith is thankful when it makes a petition of God, knowing that He is going to answer, and fervent faith is thankful when the promise manifests. Fervent faith is thankful at all times. But the Bible warns that in the last days, people will be lovers of their own selves, covetous, boasters, proud, blasphemers, disobedient to parents, unthankful, unholy, without natural affection, trucebreakers, false accusers, incontinent, fierce, despisers of those that are good, traitors, heady, highminded, and lovers of pleasures more than lovers of God (2 Timothy 3).

Does it at all strike you that the Holy Ghost lumped ingratitude in with all these other sins? It should. Ingratitude is a sin. You can't have a fervent spirit, you can't have a fiery faith walk, if you aren't overflowing with gratitude. His praise should continuously be on our lips. How sad is it that we often do more complaining than we do thanking.

The only reason we have a right to pray, the only reason we have a right to the blessings of God, the only reason we deserve anything other than hell fire is because God, in His mercy, sent Jesus Christ to take our sin upon Him that we might be saved. If you maintain a constant realize of this fact, you'll walk humbly, you'll walk thankfully, and you'll walk fervently. Need some help? Read the psalms.

> Praise the Lord! Oh, give thanks to the Lord, for He is good! For His mercy endures forever. Who can utter the mighty acts of the Lord? Who can declare all His praise?

> Psalm 106:1-2

Oh, that men would give thanks to the Lord for His goodness, And for His wonderful works to the children of men! For He satisfies the longing soul, And fills the hungry soul with goodness.

Psalm 107:8-9

So what are you waiting for? Praise God's name in song and glorify Him with thanksgiving (Psalm 69:30). Enter His gates with thanksgiving and His courts with praise; give thanks to Him and praise His name (Psalm 100:4). If you don't praise Him, the rocks will cry out.

CHAPTER 13
Rejoice Evermore

Rejoice in the Lord alway: and again I say, Rejoice.

Philippians 4:4

Rejoice. That was the only word to describe my state. I was all alone in a small holding cell wearing an oversized, bright orange jump suit that donned the word a single word across the back, "INMATE." My fellow inmates – the prostitutes, drug addicts, shoplifters and alleged petty thieves – joined hands in prayer. Like me, their only hope was God Almighty. Most of them weren't seeking justice, though. They were seeking mercy.

One by one, the women saw the judge. Some came back crying over their sentence. Others came back rejoicing over their freedom. I was waiting for my turn – and I had been waiting a long time. Eventually, it was just me and the four walls of the holding cell. I had counted every brick on the wall, every crack in the tile. It was just me and the Holy Ghost.

Long story short I had been falsely accused of a crime I didn't commit. The District Attorney wanted to send me to the Big House for five years. I had a three-year-old daughter whose 30-year-old daddy had just run off to Latin America to marry an 18-year-old girl he knocked up on a foreign assignment. My attorney had collected $70,000 in cash only to tell me to prepare to plea for something less than five years in prison. The only hope we had was that God really was a God of justice.

I was confident in Him. In fact, I refused to cast away my confidence. I had a praying grandmother in agreement with me and the Lord had already revealed the day of my release – the 40th day. Despite obstacle after delay after hindrance, I sat in that holding cell awaiting my day in court. It came on the 40th day. As I sat there all alone, waiting, I just keep thanking God by faith. That's all I knew to do.

Then it happened. After what seemed like an eternity – in fact it had been most of the day – a guard came into the holding cell to pull me into a little glass-encased room with a phone. My attorney – a new attorney my grandmother had hired on my behalf – was on the other end of the line. He had just come out of the judge's chambers. The same judge that refused twice to give me bail – even with an ankle bracelet and an agreement for house arrest.

As I listened to his voice, time seemed to stand still. He seemed to be speaking in slow motion, but he sounded thrilled. His words? "I just spoke to the judge. You won't be having your day in court." There was a short pause. Short enough for me to run through at least five different scenarios. But before I could settle on one, my attorney piped back up again, "The judge is suspending the case. You'll be home in a few hours."

Even though I expected liberty, I didn't expect it under those terms. I was shocked. I expected to have to face the judge, bite my tongue and let my attorney prove my case. It didn't go down that way. God intervened on my behalf. I didn't have to stand before my false accuser. I didn't have to listen once more to the lies launched against me. I didn't have to defend myself or even sit back and watch my attorney defend me. God proved to be my Vindicator. His justice and His mercy prevailed.

When I hung up the phone, I was at the same time thrilled and stunned. I had been sore mistreated during those 40 days, but God… I had lost just about every penny of my savings, but God… I had been separated from my baby, who had already been abandoned by her daddy, for 40 days, but God… God was turning it around. God had delivered. God was going to repay. God was going to heal. God was going to restore. I knew that this was just the beginning of a brand new season – and I knew that one day I would return to the jail to bring Jesus to people who, whether innocent or guilty, needed Christ in them, the hope of glory.

The officer escorted me back to the holding cell. As soon as she locked me in, I rejoiced. Even though I was still incarcerated, I rejoiced and rejoiced some more. With tears flowing, I uttered the same three words over and over and over again out of my mouth, "Thank you, Jesus. Thank you, Jesus. Thank you, Jesus. Thank you, Jesus." I jumped up and down. I ran around the cell. I kneeled to the floor. I lifted up my hands. I raised my voice. I kept rejoicing until I was utterly exhausted, and then I laid down on the cold, cement bench and rejoiced some more. I was on fire for God and that fire never waned – and it never will.

GET READY TO REJOICE

Maybe you don't have a story that's as dramatic as mine. Or maybe you have one that's more dramatic. It doesn't matter. That's not the point at all. The point is this: If you want to stay on fire for God, you don't need a dramatic deliverance to spark the flame. And if you do, then consider this: You've already had one. God saved you from an eternal prison of fire. For this, we should be rejoicing constantly. Rejoicing in the Lord helps us maintain a fervent spirit.

If you read the Scriptures, you'll notice that King David and the Apostle Paul had something very interesting in common: they rejoiced all the time. I don't know of two men who were more on fire for

God than David and Paul. We can learn by their example – and we are about to.

So many times we get focused on life's daily challenges and, instead of rejoicing in the God of all things possible, we complain about the devil, our circumstances and the people around us. David and Paul had plenty to complain about, if any of us do. They were both betrayed. David was rejected. Paul was beaten. You get the idea. But they knew God, His kindness, His covenant, His power – they knew Him. And they rejoiced in the God of their salvation.

DO YOU *REALLY* BELIEVE?

The Lord expects us to rejoice in Him. When we complain about anything, it's really a subtle complaint against God for allowing us to experience a circumstance we'd rather avoid. Instead of complaining, we need to take authority over the enemy, thank God for who He is, and start stepping towards the solution to the problem in faith.

When it comes to overcoming problems – whether it's financial, health, relationships or something else – we have a part to play and God has a part to play. Once you get the devil out of the scene, you need to do what you can do to resolve your problems. You need to look for that job. You need to take care of that body. You need to walk in love with your family. God will meet you in your faithful obedience to His Word. He'll give you strategies. He'll give you favor. He'll move on your behalf. But you need to rejoice before you see Him move. You need to stay on fire even when life's fire hoses are drenching you with a thousand gallons of high-pressure water that blinds your eyes and stings your skin.

One time I was dealing with a health issue. It was persistent. Obstinate might be a better word. I believed God and believed God and believed God some more. I was starting to get discouraged, so I asked God what was going on. Do you want to know what He said to me? "Act like you'd be acting if you'd already received the healing." I didn't have to think about that one too long. If I received my healing I'd be rejoicing. That's evidence of our faith because the Bible says, "What things soever ye desire, when ye pray, believe that ye receive them, and ye shall have them" (Matthew 11:24). If we believe we receive, we'll be thankful. We'll rejoice.

REJOICING WITH DAVID

Rejoicing is a running theme throughout the Bible. God expects us to rejoice. I believe He knows that rejoicing helps us maintain a fervent spirit. That's why He said, "rejoice in all that ye put your hand until, ye and your households, wherein the Lord thy God hath blessed thee" (Deuteronomy 12:7). And again, "And thou shalt rejoice in every good thing which the Lord thy God hath given unto thee" (Deuteronomy 26:11). The heart of them that seek the Lord should rejoice (1 Chronicles 16:10). Consider what the psalmist said about rejoicing:

Serve the Lord with fear, and rejoice with trembling (Psalm 2:11).

But let all those that put their trust in thee rejoice: let them ever shout for joy, because thou defendest them: let them also that love thy name be joyful in thee (Psalm 5:11).

I will be glad and rejoice in thee: I will sing praise to thy name, O thou most High (Psalm 9:2).

That I may shew forth all thy praise in the gates of the daughter of Zion: I will rejoice in thy salvation (Psalm 9:14).

But I have trusted in thy mercy; my heart shall rejoice in thy salvation (Psalm 13:5).

Rejoice in the Lord, O ye righteous: for praise is comely for the upright (Psalm 33:1).

REJOICE IN THE LORD ALWAYS

That's just the tip of the joyful iceberg. David rejoiced, rejoiced and rejoiced some more throughout the Book of Psalms. He left us an example – and that example apparently left quite an impression on the Apostle Paul, who picked up where David left off.

Paul offered some apostolic instruction with regard to rejoicing. He said:

Rejoice in hope of the glory of God (Romans 5:2).
Rejoice with them that do rejoice (Romans 12:15).
Rejoice, ye Gentiles, with his people (Romans 15:10).
Rejoiceth in the truth (1 Corinthians 13:6).
Rejoice in the day of Christ (Philippians 2:16).
Rejoice with me (Philippians 2:18).
Rejoice in the Lord (Philippians 3:1).
Rejoice in Christ Jesus (Philippians 3:3).
Rejoice in the Lord always (Philippians 4:4).
Rejoice evermore (1 Thessalonians 5:16).

Why did Paul rejoice even in his sufferings? (Colossians 1:24)? Why did he rejoice even when Christ was preached in pretence (Philippians 1:18)? Why would Paul rejoice if he was offered upon the sacrifice and service of our faith (Philippians 2:7)? And why did Paul instruct believers over and over again to rejoice? Because Paul knew a great secret: a rejoicing spirit is a fervent spirit. And a rejoicing spirit is a strong spirit because the Bible says the joy of the Lord is our strength (Nehemiah 8:10).

REJOICING WITH JESUS

Jesus also spoke of rejoicing. His words offer us a different perspective on rejoicing. They teach us to do the opposite of what our emotions may be telling us to do. A fervent spirit overcomes unhealthy emotions every time. A fervent spirit won't wallow in depression. A fervent spirit won't linger in grief. A fervent spirit won't ride the emotional rollercoaster. A fervent spirit is stable, strong and ready to serve the Lord. Consider the words of our Savior:

> Blessed are ye, when men shall revile you, and persecute you, and shall say all manner of evil against you falsely, for my sake. Rejoice, and be exceeding glad: for great is your reward in heaven: for so persecuted they the prophets which were before you.
>
> Matthew 5:11-12

You may not feel blessed when someone reviles you. I've had to train my flesh to get in agreement with my spirit in the face of persecution. The gut instinct is to retaliate. But the Jesus instinct is to turn the other cheek, to bless your enemies, and to pray for them.

Jesus also taught us to rejoice about the right things. Emotions will rejoice over things that have no lasting value in the Kingdom. Those same emotions will drag you into a pit when something goes wrong. The right things are the Kingdom of God and His righteousness. For example, we should rejoice in our eternal salvation.

> Behold, I give unto you power to tread on serpents and scorpions, and over all the power of the enemy: and nothing shall by any means hurt you.

Notwithstanding in this rejoice not, that the spirits are subject unto you; but rather rejoice, because your names are written in heaven. In that hour Jesus rejoiced in spirit, and said, I thank thee, O Father, Lord of heaven and earth, that thou hast hid these things from the wise and prudent, and hast revealed them unto babes: even so, Father; for so it seemed good in thy sight.

Luke 10:19-21

We should exercise our authority, to be sure, but we should rejoice in the One who gave it to us. Let me put it this way: We shouldn't merely rejoice in the manifestation of the devil's defeat when we bind him in the name of Jesus. We should moreover rejoice in the one Who already defeated Him. If we rejoice in the authority or its manifestation alone, we'll be disappointed the first time we don't see the results we expected. But if we rejoice, rather, in the One who gave us the authority, we'll never be disappointed. We'll be so fervent in spirit that we'll get the attention of God and the devil. God will be compelled to move on our behalf and the devil will be forced to move out of the way. Rejoice!

Again with the eternal perspective, Jesus said we should rejoice in the work of evangelism. "Say not ye, There are yet four months, and then cometh harvest?

behold, I say unto you, Lift up your eyes, and look on the fields; for they are white already to harvest. And he that reapeth receiveth wages, and gathereth fruit unto life eternal: that both he that soweth and he that reapeth may rejoice together" (John 4:35-37).

So what are you waiting for? Rejoice with joy unspeakable and full of glory (1 Peter 1:8). Rejoice, inasmuch as ye are partakers of Christ's sufferings; that, when His glory shall be revealed, ye may be glad also with exceeding joy (1 Peter 4:13). Let us be glad and rejoice, and give honor to Him (Revelation 19:7).

CHAPTER 14
The Danger of Drifting Away

Therefore we ought to give the more earnest heed to things which we have heard, lest at any time we should let them slip.

Hebrews 2:1

The danger of drifting away. I'll never forget the first time I heard Kathryn Kuhlman minister on this topic with her Missouri cornbread style. This was one of those messages that she herself admitted was more like castor oil than cornbread. A hard word, but a word in due season for many.

She based her heart to heart talk on Hebrews 2:1. It was a solemn warning to pay attention to the truth that we have heard, lest we drift away from the Lord Jesus Christ. Let's review the whole passage:

Therefore we ought to give the more earnest heed to the things which we have heard, lest at any time we should let them slip. For if the word spoken by angels was stedfast, and every transgression and disobedience received a just recompence of reward; How shall we escape, if we neglect so great salvation; which at the first began to be spoken by the Lord, and was confirmed unto us by them that heard him...

Hebrews 2:1-3

Drifting away is a danger for every believer. To drift is to become driven or carried along; to move along a line of least resistance; to move in a random or casual way; to become carried along subject to no guidance or control; or to vary or deviate from a set course of adjustment.

Think of a balloon that floats smoothly and effortlessly through the air. The balloon is driven or carried along. That happens because the balloon is not putting up any resistance to the wind. It moves in a random way. You can't predict which way it will go next – and you can't control it. Even if you set it on a course, it's prone to deviate from that path because it's drifting.

LOT LINGERS IN SODOM

Now let's talk about drifting in human terms. Drifting is subtle. If it were noticeable, most would resist it at its onset. But drifting off the narrow path is often hardly noticeable at first. It starts with little foxes, small sins that seem negligible. Of course, no sin is negligible. But it seems some sin is more socially acceptable. This in itself is a deception. The sin of drug use is no worse than the sin of jealousy. When we fellowship with the spirit of the world, we'll begin to drift away.

Jesus said the gate is wide, and the way is broad that leads to destruction (Matthew 7:13). It's not too hard to find the wide gate or to enter into it. If we don't make a concerted daily effort to stay on the narrow path, we'll subtly drift toward that broad way. If we want to stay rooted and grounded in Christ, we have to abide in His Word and let His Word abide in us. We have to develop a relationship – we have to actively pursue it.

Look at Lot. When he separated from Abraham, he first moved his tent as far as Sodom. Sodom is associated with shameless sinning (Isaiah 3:9). Sodom and its neighboring city Gomorrah is connected to adultery and lies (Jeremiah 23:14). Sodom is the epitome of careless living (Luke 17:28-29). Sodom and Gomorrah, and the cities around them, gave themselves over to fornication and going after strange flesh (Jude 1:7).

If Lot didn't know this when he chose the valley of the Jordan, where Sodom called home, then it certainly didn't take him long to figure it out. Yet he decided to stay in Sodom and even sat in the gate of Sodom. Only people of authority and influence sat in the gate of a city. Lot had drifted away from righteousness and into Sin City. When angels urged him to leave the Sodom, the Bible says he lingered there. His wife even looked back on the sinful city, and turned into a pillar of salt. Then his daughters got Lot drunk and committed incest. The sin of Sodom was manifest in Lot's family even after they escaped the fire and brimstone.

PARALYZED BY SIN

I read a story one time by an unknown author. It was about a little bird who was enjoying a ride down the river toward Niagara Falls. The bird was floating downstream on a piece of wood without a care in the world. The little bird never considered any possibility of danger. That's because the little bird had a plan. When it got near the falls, it would simply fly away.

The little bird relaxed on the piece of wood that carried it effortlessly toward the edge of the falls. Just before the piece of wood was about to plummet into the waterfall, the little bird tried to flap its wings. But something went wrong. The mist from the river caused the little bird's wings to freeze up. The bird could not escape the rushing waters of Niagara and died in the waters.

Sometimes we get involved with people or projects we know we should break free from. The Holy Ghost tries to warn us in a still small voice, but the voice of our flesh drowns out the Spirit. And so we drift away from Christ down the river to destruction. Don't think it couldn't happen to you. If it happened to well-known leaders in the Body of Christ who were known for helping millions, it can happen to you or me.

The Bible says we have to work out our salvation with fear and trembling (Philippians 2:12). We cannot look on the warnings of God with indifference. We cannot live out of a double mind, looking like a saint on Sunday and living like the devil the rest of the week, or even for a few minutes of one day. We have to always consider Christ and His will and His ways.

> What I'm getting at, friends, is that you should simply keep on doing what you've done from the beginning. When I was living among you, you lived in responsive obedience. Now that I'm separated from you, keep it up. Better yet, redouble your efforts. Be energetic in your life of salvation, reverent and sensitive before God.

Philippians 2:12-13

ONCE SAVED, ALWAYS SAVED?

Again, the Bible clearly states that there is a danger of drifting away if we do not pay close attention to the Word of truth. The writer of Hebrews was speaking to born again believers. This wasn't a message that ended in a salvation call to sinners. This was a message that exhorted believers not to neglect the Gospel of our salvation.

Think about it for a minute. What happens when you neglect to eat healthy foods and exercise? You gain unwanted weight. What happens if you neglect to brush your teeth? You get cavities and eventually, if you don't change your habits, your teeth will rot out. What happens if you neglect to show up to work on time? If you practice lateness, you'll probably get fired.

The point I am driving at is this: nothing good comes from neglect. There are no positive consequences associated with neglect. Consider the very meaning of the word. Neglect means to disregard. Disregard means to pay no attention to or to treat as unworthy of respect or attention.

So what do you think will happen if we neglect our salvation? if we aren't motivated to action based on His sacrifice? if we treat the Gospel as unworthy of our respect and attention? I submit to you that we'll get fleshly, our spiritual zeal will decay and we'll lose our place in the Kingdom.

Jesus Himself speaks of blotting names out of the Book of Life (Revelation 3:2, 5). Jesus also speaks of those who have prophesied in His name and cast out devils in His name and done many wonderful works in His name who did not make it through the narrow gate (Matthew 7:21-22).

DO YOU GET MY DRIFT?

Rather than debating doctrine, though, let's look at what it means to drift away and how it begins. Balloons drift. They float along effortlessly, carried along by the wind. But Christians should not drift. Even the Christian walk is not one in which we're carried. We have to make a conscious decision to walk by faith and it requires effort. The Holy Spirit leads us, and may even help pull us along at times, but He's not going to drive us toward out destination like a balloon floating in the air without any will of its own.

When I think about the danger of drifting away, a Scripture from the book of Ephesians comes to mind. The Apostle Paul is talking about how Jesus gave gifts to men, some apostles, some prophets, some evangelists, some pastors and teachers for the perfecting of the saints for the work of the ministry (Ephesians 4:11). We often stop there but the thought continues:

> Till we all come in the unity of the faith, and of the knowledge of the Son of God, unto a perfect man, unto the measure of the stature of the fulness of Christ: That

we henceforth be no more children, tossed to and fro, and carried about with every wind of doctrine, by the sleight of men, and cunning craftiness, whereby they lie in wait to deceive...

Ephesians 4:13-14

You might say it this way: falling under the influence of false doctrines designed by the devil to deceive you. We must pay close attention to the Gospel truth we've heard lest the winds of deceitful doctrines sway us. These include secular humanism and New Age mysticism, both of which have subtly crept into the Church of Jesus Christ.

DECEITFUL DOCTRINES

The doctrine of secular humanism manifests as selfishness. The secular humanist feels good about himself regardless of his behavior and masks his guilt with a positive confession. His goal is to gain as much happiness and material wealth as he can. His morals have no absolutes. When you are seeking to please yourself without thought of God and fellow man, you are being carried away by this deceitful doctrine. It's an anti-Christ doctrine masked as tolerance whose tentacles are reaching into the Church.

Then there's New Age mysticism. In the New Age movement, you are a god. Animals are gods. Plants, water and dirt are gods. Salvation involves enlightenment through occult practices and human works like yoga, meditation and altered states of consciousness rather than through Jesus Christ. Death is merely an illusion. New Age mysticism often manifests itself through prophetic ministry in the form of super-spiritual dreams and visions or through an adulterated faith message, where positive affirmations become a reality.

I believe strongly in the prophetic and in the truths we learned in the faith movement. But New Age perverts both. New Age offers inklings of truth – doctrines that sound on the surface like truth – but these doctrines lie in wait to deceive, denying the Lord Jesus Christ and His sacrifice as the only means to salvation.

That's why the restoration of the entire five-fold ministry is so vital to the Church today. The Bible says Jesus gave us apostles, prophets, evangelists, pastors and teachers to equip us for our assignment, to bring unity to the Body, to help us mature – and to prevent us from drifting into false teachings that are so subtle that those who aren't paying close attention to the Gospel of our salvation might slip into them.

TRUTH OR CONSEQUENCES?

Remember Finney? We studied one of his sermons in Chapter 2. In that lesson, we looked at the consequences of obeying the requirement to put on Christ. In the light of our text in this chapter, I thought it expedient to look at Finney's take on the consequences of disobeying this requirement to put on the Lord Jesus Christ and make no provision for the flesh, to fulfill its lusts (Romans 13:14). So let's go back once again to March 15, 1843 and receive this warning in the spirit in which it was given:

> If you are a professor of religion, you will be a hypocrite, and people will know it. There are, perhaps, some, who are successful in keeping on the mask. But most, betray themselves sooner or later, and are known in their true character.
>
> You will render peace of mind impossible. You will render yourself justly despicable. All love to see men live up to their profession, and naturally cry out against hypocrisy.
>
> You will ruin your own soul, and do the most you can to ruin others.
>
> You will bring upon yourself the endless execration of all beings in the Universe, both good and bad.

In case you are wondering what execration means, it's a 14th century word for a curse. Finny isn't saying here that God will curse you. Rather he is saying you will be a curse among men. People will detest you – and you probably won't like yourself too much, either. There's few things worse than living a life of regret.

COUNTING THE COSTS

Thank God, He always lets us choose blessing or curses (Deuteronomy 28). So as we close this chapter, let's look at the blessings of putting on Christ, of staying fervent in spirit, of being on fire for God. And let us keep in mind the big picture: Eternity. Because there's a price to pay to live for Christ, but when you pay that price you also receive great blessings in exchange. Let's listen in on Finney's lecture one last time.

1. The first consequence I mention, is, you will have much opposition. You can expect no better usage than Christ received. "It is enough for the servant that he be as his master."

2. You may expect great trials. This is the inheritance of all who will live godly in Christ Jesus. Look at Paul. While he was a Pharisee, he went on smoothly. The gales of popular favor swelled his sails. But when he became the preacher of the cross, ah! then he knew what it was to go against wind and tide.

3. Men will accuse you of having a bad spirit. They have always brought this charge against the true followers of Christ, and especially against Christ Himself. He said so much about their teachers, creeds, and traditions, and rebuked them so plainly, that they finally tried, and executed him as a blasphemer.

4. You will need great meekness, and at the same time great decision of character. Without both of these qualities, you cannot endure the shock of a world arrayed against you.

5. You will subject yourself to much misapprehension. Men will not understand you. Many wonder, why Christians are so misunderstood. But it is not at all wonderful. Who was ever more misunderstood than Jesus Christ? The simple fact is, a selfish mind does not understand the principle upon which a true Christian acts.

6. If you are misunderstood, you will of course, be misrepresented. This you must expect.

7. It will subject you to the loss of many friends. They will think you are ultra, extravagant, and carrying matters too far. And every new step you take, you will see an additional falling off. They will walk no more with you. But all the consequences are not evil.

THE BLESSINGS OF OBEDIENCE

After reading the first seven consequences of living a life sold out to Christ, you may be wondering if you can cut muster. Can you really stand up to that external pressure without compromise? You can if you have a zealous spirit. You can if you truly put on Christ. You can if you have fervent faith. Jeremiah and Job both endured much worse than most of us will ever face. So did many of the apostles of the Lamb. And they were all blessed beyond measure.

Before we return to the 21ˢᵗ Century, I want to with a few final thoughts from Finney. Namely, the consequences for obeying the command to put on Christ. Finney would know all to well the consequences for putting on Christ for He walked in Him to a degree to which many Christians never attain. Let's look at what we can expect when we put on Christ as spoken from the mouth of a man who helped apostle the Second Great Awakening.

1. You will inherit his peace of mind; and this is worth more than all the world can give. You will sleep just as sweetly, eat with just as much relish, and enjoy the tranquil hours just as really, as if you had all the world's favor. Persons often wonder, whether such are not unhappy. I answer, nay. They are the only persons who know what true happiness is.

2. His joy will be fulfilled in you. This is His promise; and His true followers sympathize with Him in all the joys He had.

3. You will share His glory in being the representative of the true God. Christ was sent to reveal the true character of God. He took the law which lay on tables of stone, and acted it out; thus showing mankind just what God was. Without such a manifestation, as was thus made of His true character, men must have always remained in ignorance. Every one, then, who puts on the Lord Jesus Christ, will share this glory with Him, of making known to the world the true character of God.

4. You will be able to say, with Paul, "For me to live, is Christ." The Apostle seems to have had this idea in his mind, that Christ lived his life over again in him. So it will be with you. Christ renews His life in His true followers.

5. You will be able to say from your own consciousness, as John says, "Truly our fellowship is with the Father, and with His Son Jesus Christ."

6. You will be happy in the highest degree of which you are capable in this life. And you will be no less useful, than you are happy.

Oh, what a marvelous existence.

CHAPTER 15

The Holy Ghost and Fire

*I indeed baptize you in water unto repentance: but he that
cometh after me is mightier than I, whose shoes I am not worthy
to bear: he shall baptize you in the Holy Spirit ...*

Matthew 3:10-13

When John the Baptist came on the scene, he had
authority from heaven to baptize people in water unto
repentance. That's where his authority ended. But
thank God another came after Him who had the
authority to baptize in the Holy Spirit – Jesus Christ.

I believe if we hope to maintain fervent spirit and
fervent faith, we need the power of the Holy Ghost in
our lives. I believe effectiveness in ministry is
diminished without the in-filling of the Holy Spirit.

RESPONDING TO THE FIRE

The fire of God played a key role in the live of many great men and women of God, from Abraham to David to Solomon to Elijah and beyond.

God spoke to Moses from a flame of fire out of the midst of a bush (Exodus 3:2). When Moses saw the fire, he could have kept walking. But he stopped to take a closer look. When God noticed that Moses turned to see, He called him into his destiny. What will you do when you see the fire of God? Will you press in and enter your destiny? Or will you hurriedly walk by without a second look? When the fire of God comes, we must recognize it, embrace it, and let it do its work in us.

The nation of Israel was led through the wilderness by a pillar of fire at night. The fire of God will lead you through your wilderness, too. How long it takes you to make your way through that wilderness depends, in part, on how you respond to the fire. The Holy Ghost is not your spiritual tour guide. You can't complain when you don't like the itinerary or the accommodations. That's what the Israelites did. They did not reverence the fire; they did not reverence His presence or His leadership. And a generation died in the desert.

David understood the fire of God, and he knew that sometimes God answers by fire. David was willing to pay the price to sacrifice to his God. David built an altar unto the Lord, and offered burnt offerings and peace offerings, and called upon the Lord. The Bible says God answered him from heaven by fire upon the altar of burnt offerings (1 Chronicles 21:26). In this instance, the fire of God showed forth the mercy of God to forgive David for his transgression of numbering Israel.

Solomon experienced the fire of God in the wake of prayer. It got the attention of a nation.

> Now when Solomon had made an end of praying, the fire came down from heaven, and consumed the burnt offering and the sacrifices; and the glory of the Lord filled the house.
>
> And the priests could not enter into the house of the Lord, because the glory of the Lord had filled the Lord's house.
>
> And when all the children of Israel saw how the fire came down, and the glory of the Lord upon the house, they bowed themselves with their faces to the ground upon the pavement, and worshipped, and praised the Lord, saying, For he is good; for his mercy endureth for ever. Then the king and all the people offered sacrifices before the Lord.
>
> 2 Chronicles 7:1-4

Can you see the response to the glory of God falling? The people weren't concerned about a chicken in the oven or the crowd building at Denny's. When the people saw God moving, they worshipped and praised Him. This is the only appropriate response. If we don't reverence the presence of God, what do we reverence? If you want to stay on fire for God – and increase that fire – then be sensitive to His presence.

REFINED BY FIRE

If you want truly fervent faith, you may need to submit to the refiner's fire and the testing by fire. Fire has a purifying element to it. Fire burns up impurities. So if you aren't able to maintain a fervent spirit – if you can't seem to stay on fire for God when the winds blow and the storms rage – then it's possible you need the refiner's fire to work out of you the impurities that hinder your faith. Consider the words of Peter the apostle:

> [You should] be exceedingly glad on this account, though now for a little while you may be distressed by trials and suffer temptations,
>
> So that [the genuineness] of your faith may be tested, [your faith] which is infinitely more precious than the perishable gold which is tested and purified by fire. [This proving of your faith is intended] to redound to [your]

praise and glory and honor when Jesus
Christ (the Messiah, the Anointed
One) is revealed.

1 Peter 1:6-7 (AMP)

You can't fake it 'til you make it when it comes to
your faith walk. Not only will the genuineness of your
faith be tested, but the genuineness of your works will
also be tested. If we aren't serving as unto the Lord –
if we have motivations that aren't pleasing to God
such as man-pleasing or self-promotion – then those
works won't count for anything in the end. In a letter
to the church at Corinth, Paul wrote:

> The work of each [one] will become
> [plainly, openly] known (shown for
> what it is); for the day [of Christ] will
> disclose and declare it, because it will
> be revealed with fire, and the fire will
> test and critically appraise the character
> and worth of the work each person has
> done.
>
> If the work which any person has built
> on this Foundation [any product of his
> efforts whatever] survives [this test], he
> will get his reward.
>
> But if any person's work is burned up
> [under the test], he will suffer the loss
> [of it all, losing his reward], though he

himself will be saved, but only as [one who has passed] through fire.

1 Corinthians 3:13-15 (AMP)

If you want to become white hot with passion for the Lord, if you need a spark, if you need to rekindle that love, ask the Lord to fill you to overflowing with His Holy Spirit. Why not pray right now before you close the pages on this book? Pray with me:

Father God, I come to you in the name of Jesus. I thank you that you sent your only begotten Son to save me and I thank you that you desire to fill me with your Holy Spirit. Jesus said, "How much more shall your heavenly Father give the Holy Spirit to those who ask Him." Right now, I ask you in the name of Jesus to fill me with your Holy Spirit. I receive the indwelling of your Spirit right now and I confess by faith that I am Spirit-filled. I thank you that You have given me a prayer language to communicate with you and I yield my tongue to your Spirit right now. I expect to speak in tongues as the Spirit gives me utterance. I thank you and praise you. Amen!

ABOUT THE AUTHOR

Jennifer LeClaire is a prophetic voice and teacher whose passion is to see the lost come to Christ and equip believers to understand the will and ways of God. She carries a reforming voice that seeks to turn hearts to the Lord and edify the Body of Christ.

Jennifer has a powerful testimony of God's power to set the captives free and claim beauty for ashes. She shares her story with women who need to understand the love and grace of God in a lost and dying world.

Jennifer is news editor at Charisma magazine. Some of her work is archived in the Flower Pentecostal Heritage Museum. Her materials have been translated into Spanish and Korean.

Jennifer serves as director of the International House of Prayer in Fort Lauderdale, executive pastor of Praise Chapel Hollywood and is a board member at Christ Kingdom Evangelist Network.

Jennifer is a prolific author who has written several books, including "The Heart of the Prophetic," "A Prophet's Heart," "Faith Magnified," "Did the Spirit of God Say That?," "The Spiritual Warrior's Guide to Defeating Jezebel," "The Making of a Prophet," and "Breakthrough." Her materials have been translated into Spanish and Korean.

Other Books by Jennifer LeClaire

- Faith Magnified
- Breakthrough!
- The Heart of the Prophetic: Keys to flowing in a more powerful prophetic anointing
- A Prophet's Heart: Avoiding the Doorway to Deception
- Did the Spirit of God Say That?
- The Spiritual Warrior's Guide to Defeating Jezebel
- The Making of a Prophet

Visit Jennifer online at:

www.jenniferleclaire.org

www.facebook.com/propheticbooks

www.twitter.com/propheticbooks

www.youtube.com/jnleclaire

www.flickr.com/propheticbooks

www.myspace.com/propheticbooks

www.connect.tangle.com/propheticbooks

When The Holy
Dances With
The Ordinary